M000101218

MODEL

RICK THOMAS

MODEL

The Complete Guide to Becoming a Professional Model

STEPHEN WOLTER

MARIE PHILOMENE ANDERSON

Foreword by
John Casablancas

DOUBLEDAY

NEW YORK, LONDON, TORONTO, SYDNEY, AUCKLAND

Published by Bantam Doubleday Dell Publishing Group Inc.,
666 Fifth Avenue, New York, New York 10103.
Doubleday and the portrayal of an anchor with a dolphin are trademarks
of Doubleday, a division of Bantam Doubleday Dell Publishing Group, Inc.

Library of Congress Cataloging-in-Publication Data

Anderson, Marie, 1958-
    Model : a complete guide to becoming a professional model / Marie
Anderson. — 1st ed.
        p. cm.
        ISBN 0−385−26020−2 (pbk.)
        1. Models, Fashion – United States – Vocational guidance.
    I. Title.
    HD6073. M772U528 1989   88−20295
    659. 1'52—dc 19   CIP

Canadian Cataloging-in-Publication Data
    Anderson, Marie, 1958-
        Model
    ISBN 0−385−26020−2
        1. Models, Fashion – Vocational guidance.
    I. Title.
    HD6073.M77A7 1989
    659.1'52
    C88−094905−8

ISBN 0 385 26020 2

Editor: Trish Burgess
Art Director: Anne Fisher
Managing Editor: Pippa Rubinstein

First published by Dragon's World Ltd., Limpsfield and London
© Copyright Dragon's World 1988
© Copyright text Marie P. Anderson 1988
© Copyright on hair Judith Gold 1988
© Copyright on make-up Darcy McGrath 1988
© Copyright artwork Dragon's World 1988
© Copyright in all photographs resides with the photographers
    unless otherwise specified.

Printed in Singapore
March 1989
First edition

Dedication

This book is dedicated to my special guides and teachers:

Marcelle Poirier Anderson and Bruce Anderson Jr.
William Russell Gray
Pera Marshall Odishoo
Lawrence Lee Close
Stanley Edward Malinowski Jr.
Jane Marie Stewart
Donna Surges-Tatum
Christopher Owen
Matthew Louis Amato
J. Cortland Boyd

And most of all to God! Without His strength and guidance this book would not have been possible.

In Memory of Maria Louise Caleel

PREFACE

I wrote this book because I see so many people wasting a great deal of time and money pursuing a career in modeling—a career that must be taken seriously and planned out very carefully. It is continually frustrating for me to interview people who have no idea of what they are doing.

The main emphasis of this book is on the theory and strategy of modeling. The field has become so incredibly competitive that it is only rare luck that will make you a success if you do not go about it correctly and professionally.

No other person can make the decision for you to become a model. You have to follow your own direction and not let anything stand in the way. If you are discouraged from becoming a model because of a negative review from an agency or an agent, then perhaps you do not want it badly enough. Make sure you try all of the possibilities. Over the years, I have seen many men and women become successful when negative influences could have interfered.

Being an agent is what I do best. I am not a make-up artist, hairdresser, accountant, or health and nutrition consultant. To give you the most current and thorough information in these areas I have included chapters written by established professionals—Darcy McGrath (make-up), Judith Gold (hair), Debra Lessin (finances) and Curtis Brackenbury (nutrition and exercise). They also will give you insight and encouragement along the winding road ahead.
Read, learn, and enjoy.

Marie Anderson
Chicago, 1988

CONTENTS

STEPHEN WOLTER

JOHN BECKETT

INTRODUCTION

At sixteen years of age I had no self-confidence. When circumstances forced me into seeking employment, I arranged an interview for myself as a model at a local department store. The interview was brief and I was told: "You'll never be a model — you're too tall!" I left feeling worthless and depressed, assuming that the interviewer knew more than I did.

Later, I decided to become a fashion designer. Since I had been designing my own clothes and sewing since the age of ten, I thought I had a reasonable chance of succeeding. However, when I divulged my ambition to my teacher she said, "You'll never be a designer — you don't have the talent!" Another discouraging person whom I again assumed knew more than I did.

By the time I was seventeen I was divorced and had graduated from Cocoa Beach High School in Florida. I was determined to become more than a cashier at the local grocery store, so I headed for the big city — Chicago. My first job was as a receptionist for twenty employment counselors in a secretarial agency. Eventually, I became secretary to the company president. As he was also involved in the restaurant/bar business, I acquired extensive experience in the opening and managing of these establishments. Later, I was promoted to my own counseling position.

At the age of twenty-one, I felt I had reached a peak in the placement industry. Unfamiliar with photography, but equipped with secretarial skills, counseling and management experience, I was interviewed by the international fashion photographer, Stan Malinowski. I began as his secretary, but quickly moved into managing the photo studio and his personal affairs. After three and a half years of traveling throughout Europe and the US, I became thoroughly knowledgeable of the fashion industry, but I knew there was more to learn. I decided to become a modeling agent.

I called Jane Stewart of Stewart Talent Model Management Agency and voiced my interest in the business. Within a few weeks I was working for her as the booker of female models, hairstylists and make-up artists. Six months later, the company merged with John Casablancas to form Elite Chicago Model Management Agency. (Stewart Talent became a separate agency representing children and commercial talent.) Two years later I was promoted to director of Elite Chicago. Since 1986 I have been vice-president of the agency.

In response to the need for current education about the modeling industry, Jane Stewart and John Casablancas opened the John Casablancas Career Development Center in Chicago in 1985. As I progressed through the agency, I began teaching my own class: "The Business of Modelling". My counseling work in the secretarial agency had taught me how to prepare people for interviews, my work with Stan Malinowski had given me experience of foreign travel and prestigious clients—Valentino, Clinique, Vogue and Cosmopolitan to name just a few. I also worked with celebrities, including Iman, Christie Brinkley, Cheryl Teigs and Lesley-Anne Down. This provided me with a marvellous education about the up-market fashion industry. Back in Chicago, I was able to learn the catalogue market through working with such companies as K-Mart, Evans, Marshall Fields, Sears and Montgomery Ward. Drawing on my various areas of experience, I have taught many people how to become successful models. The majority had no concept of the business, but together we made magic in their lives.

Having been told twice in my life, "You can't!", I approach interviews with aspiring and established models rather differently. I treat them as if I am looking at myself as a teenager—I have empathy. Over the past year and a half, I have been told, "You can't write a book!" Fortunately I knew better than to listen to such negative comments. I believed in myself and as a result you are now reading my first attempt at authorship!

The following letter is from Marianne Hoerner, a young model with writing experience who assisted me in editing my original manuscript. After completing her assignment with me, she left for Europe to continue her modeling career. Months later, she returned home and called me. Upon hearing of her experiences, I suggested that she pass on her thoughts to you.

"When Marie first approached me to help her write this book, I was a newcomer to the modeling world. Not only was it an opportunity to acquire more writing and editing experience, it was a great crash course in the modeling profession. After three months of working on the book, I set off to Milan and my first taste of full-time modeling *and* a European market. I can't begin to tell you the value of the knowledge I gained from Marie. It gave me an informed perspective and helped me survive those 'special' experiences that can only be lived through rather than read about.

Modeling is overwhelming at first, isn't it? But it gets better each step of the way. Every little bit of experience I gain gives me more confidence. And yet, there are times when I feel I just can't give any more — but I have to, if modeling is what I want to do. And I can't let any of that struggle show. I must remember that my job is to present myself as a product I believe in.

Everything takes time, and every career requires its own unique sacrifices. Modeling is so highly glamorized that aspiring models often don't realize the work involved. Very few are picked off the streets and put on the newsstands. In the ten months I have been in the business I have seen and been one of the many girls who gets frustrated when things don't happen quickly. Don't give up! But do remember that this is your career — you can't depend on anyone else to do the work for you. You have to hustle. And most importantly, you have to walk with your eyes open. "

Marianne Hoerner
International Model

12

FOREWORD

Modeling is without any doubt, the glamour profession of the 1980s. I am in a better position than most to know how eager aspiring models (and their parents) are to get clear answers to the many questions they have about this not-very-well-known profession. I also know how frustrated they become because ill-informed "experts" and incomplete publications provide them with only partial or inaccurate information.

When Marie Anderson told me about her book project, I was immediately supportive, knowing how varied her experience in the field of modeling has been and how professional and thorough she is at everything she does. Most books about modeling address the subject in a very general way. The fundamental problems, such as finding the right agency, knowing how to handle oneself and how to survive at the very beginning when income is still low, seem to be the major preoccupations of the aspiring model.

I met Marie in Rome, Italy, many years ago when she was running top photographer Stan Malinowski's studio. Some years after, when I became a partner of Jane Stewart to create and launch Elite Chicago, I was particularly delighted to count Marie Anderson as one of our principal collaborators.

As a manager of models' careers, and as Elite Chicago's Director of Administration, Marie deals on a daily basis with the multitude of problems that beginner and young, upcoming models have to cope with. As an executive, she has first-hand access to information on what is happening in New York, Tokyo, Paris, London, Milan and many other major cities where Elite has offices. As an experienced professional in practically every area of the modeling/fashion/beauty and photography fields, she can provide wide-ranging views on the best paths to choose from to attain success.

Marie Anderson has been intimately involved with the launching and developing of some of today's top modeling stars (Cindy Crawford being the most recent and shining example). However, what makes me truly believe that her book offers the best and most comprehensive advice is that she sincerely feels close to "her" models and is convinced that modeling is actually a school of life: the discipline, knowledge, and attitudes acquired during the formation of a model are invaluable in any other business or social context.

John Casablancas
Chicago, 1988

CHAPTER 1

HOW TO GET AN AGENCY

Finding your niche

•

Getting an interview

•

The interview

DAN ZAITZ

Agents are constantly on the lookout for new models and have been known to pick potential talent out of the crowd. More frequently, though, it takes hard work and dedication to become a successful model.

Whether you become a model or an astronaut it is important to know that only you can decide your destiny—not your parents, brother or sister, boyfriend or girlfriend, aunts or uncles. You have to follow your own direction and dreams and not allow anything to stand in the way. You have to decide if you have the potential to become a model. It is up to the agents to decide if they want to represent you. How can an agent possibly know what you are capable of doing?

FINDING YOUR NICHE

There are several types of modeling agency each representing various model types. Each agency has an image it tries to project and maintain. Every model represented by the agency is an extension of its image. What is your image? What kind of model could you be?

Women: Are you 5ft 8in or taller? Do you weigh 110–120lb? Do you measure 34B–24–34? Do you wear a size 6–8?

Men: Are you 5ft 11in–6ft 1in tall? Do you weigh 155–180lb? Do you measure 40–32–38? Do you wear size 40R?

Do you resemble any of the models in the fashion magazines? Do you have clear, evenly-toned skin? Do you have even, white teeth?

If you have answered yes to several of these questions, then perhaps you could become a print fashion and/or runway model.

If you are shorter and heavier than a straight-size model you may fit into a more specialized market of "full figure" or "petite" modeling. (These categories do not exist for male models.)

Do you have great hands, feet or legs? Perhaps you could become a "part" model.

This chapter concentrates on print fashion modeling (known as photographic modeling in the UK).

GETTING AN INTERVIEW

As all agencies do not represent all ages and sizes, it is imperative to know which agency to see and why. You could begin by going through the telephone book and calling all the modeling agencies listed, or asking other models and photographers for referrals.

Be prepared for brisk treatment when calling an agency. Remember the receptionist has to deal with hundreds of calls from clients, agents, photographers, models, messengers and hopefuls all needing immediate attention. If the receptionist sounds abrupt, do not take it personally. You can always ask the best time to call back so your questions can be answered more fully. An initial

> **"** If models want to have pictures shot before they go see agencies, they should make them natural; use Elle magazine as a guide. **"**
> Peter McClafferty
> Agent

telephone enquiry to an agency might go as follows:

Receptionist: Good morning, Models International, may I help you?
Caller: Yes, I am interested in becoming a model. How can I arrange an interview with your agency?
Receptionist: (Will give a short explanation)

or

Receptionist: Good morning, John Williamson Agency.
Caller: Good morning. I'm a new model and I'd like to arrange an interview with your agency.
Receptionist: (Will give a short explanation)

Each agency has its own system of appointments. When you call the receptionist will inform you if a personal interview can be arranged, or tell you where to send your photos. Sometimes agencies have open auditions (walk-in interviews) and the receptionist will tell you where and when to attend. Be prepared for the receptionist to decide if you are suitable for the agency and if you may see an agent. (Note that it is very unprofessional to simply turn up at an agency and expect an interview without an appointment.)

I have signed many models who have simply sent me decent snapshots. Mail your pictures or a composite with a stamped self-addressed envelope and write your name and telephone number on the back of each shot. Send whatever you can afford not to have returned. Agencies get bogged down with mail and it is very difficult to keep track of every single photo submitted. If a friend takes your photos, make sure they look like you. Your make-up should look very clean and your hairstyle should be shown; do not curl, spray or tease. Be sure to include a bathing suit shot to show the proportions of your body.

If an agency is interested in interviewing you, it will contact you by phone or mail. This could take a few weeks, so be prepared to wait.

> **"** I have signed quite a few models who have sent pictures through the mail. All they need to submit is a head shot and a body shot. Keep it very simple – minimal make-up and simply-styled hair. **"**
> Leah McCloskey
> Agent

```
Tel: (555) 123 4567          999 City Road
                             Bigtown
                             E. Maryland

                             March 23rd, 1989


Dear New Faces

My name is Jane Smith.  I am 5ft 8 inches
tall, weigh 110lb, and have blonde hair
and blue eyes.

I am interested in becoming a model and
hope you will like the snapshots I'm
enclosing.  If you are interested in
interviewing me, I am available daily after
3 P.M.

Sincerely

Jane Smith

Jane Smith
```

The letter you enclose with your snapshots should be brief and to the point, like the one shown left. First impressions are important, so make sure it is either typed neatly on white paper, or beautifully handwritten on attractive stationery.

Agents are happy to arrange an initial interview based on reasonable snapshots. Make sure you include one full-face and one full-length (preferably in a swimsuit).

17

THE INTERVIEW

It is not necessary to have a portfolio of photographs to obtain an interview. Agencies are used to making initial assessments from snapshots. A good agent can assess your marketability from looking at you in person and will tell you candidly if she can help you to pursue a career in modeling, or if you should see other agencies. (Note that agents can be male or female. For the purposes of this book, I refer to the agent as "she" throughout.) Make the most of your interview by remembering the following points.

- Being interviewed as a model is just like being interviewed for any other job; you have to sell yourself.

- Wear clean, casual clothes, choosing fitted rather than loose garments.

- Use minimal make-up and keep your hair clean and simply styled.

- Have your hands manicured. It's fine not to wear polish, but be sure to have your nails clean, filed and buffed.

- Bring whatever recent flattering pictures you may have.

- Bring paper and pen and be prepared to write down any instructions or referrals that the agent might give you. (It's so irritating when an interviewee says, "Oh, will you write that down for me?" You are asking free advice and possibly acquiring a new agency, so don't start off on the wrong foot. The agent is not your secretary.)

- Be on time. Call if you are going to be late.

- Be patient if the agent is delayed. Other business, such as photographers calling, models needing help, or unexpected emergencies must take priority. Agents first take care of the talent they represent and then go on to considering others. Your interview is a brief interlude in a busy day so make your interruption a pleasant one.

- When you meet the agent you should look into her eyes, smile and, if you wish, give a firm handshake.

- When you sit down with the agent wait for her to ask for your pictures, if you have them. Do not just assume that she will want to have them thrust at her immediately. When requested, hand over your snapshots or unfasten your portfolio and place it in the correct direction for the agent's view.

- Do not inspect or fidget with anything on the agent's desk unless you are invited to do so. Consider anything that does not belong to you or that is not handed to you as private property—no trespassing!

- If the agent should leave the desk, do not get up and walk around—it is presumptuous to assume you have free access to the environment. Sit patiently and wait for the agent to return.

One of the first questions that I ask an aspiring model is, "What do you want to accomplish from this interview with me today?"

I've heard, "I don't know what I'm doing here. I mean, you're the agent, don't you tell me?"

I've also heard, "I've been interested in becoming a fashion model for a few years and now have the money and time to try it. I also understand that Elite is the best in fashion modeling and I want to start at the top. Could you please give me the advice and direction I need?"

I became irritated with the first interviewee because she was wasting my valuable time. I was delighted with the second because she knew which agency was respected in her field and she stated her reason for being there very clearly.

"I hate when models come to an interview with their hair all foo-fooed out with more mousse than you can drown a rat in, or with so much make-up that you can't see what they look like.
Gerard Bisignano
Agent

Terrible haircuts, excess weight, bad skin, poor attitudes and unprofessional behavior can turn an agent off immediately. Personality is a major part in deciding if I'll sign a model. I assume that you will interact with clients in the same manner that you interact with me. I believe that if a model does not already know how to communicate, then it will take too long to teach her or him. I have signed many models who may not have a look that I immediately believe in, but they have sold me on their motivation and personality.

"Mothers should attend the first interview, but allow the model time alone with the agent at the beginning. If the agent is interested she or he will invite the parent to join the conversation. The parent should allow the model to speak directly to the agent. At the end of the interview the parent can ask whatever questions are on her mind.
Coral Weigel
Freelance scout

> *Leave the boyfriends at home!*
>
> Gerard Bisignano
> Agent

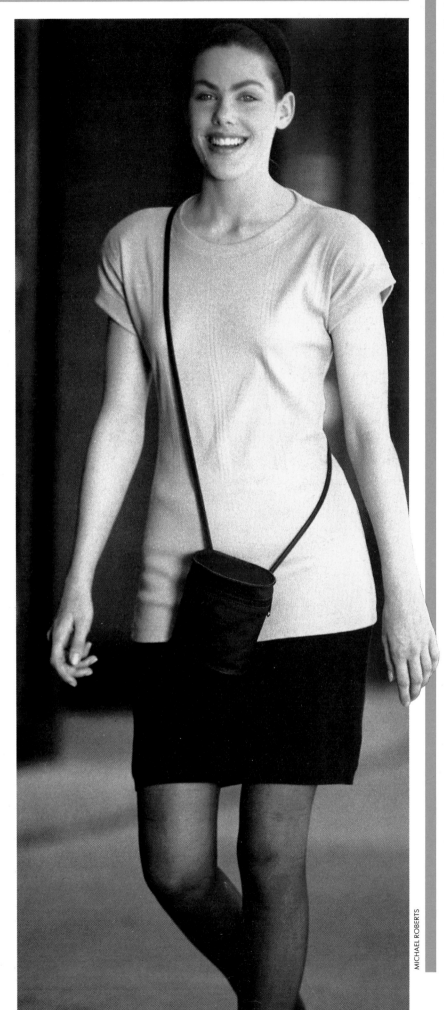

MICHAEL ROBERTS

You need to look clean, fresh and neat for an interview. Choose fitted clothes that match the image you want to project, and choose an agency that already projects your sort of image.

19

ninety six° 2925 oceanside blvd., oceanside, ca 92054 619/439-0861   photography/richard hume

Always ask questions. You must realize that you are interviewing the agent just as the agent is interviewing you. If the interviewer is not going to be your agent once you have signed up, find out who will be. You have to like and trust that person. Be very careful. You and your agent should agree on your career strategy. Here are some questions that may help you in your interview:

- How would you market me?
- How much money will I have to invest immediately and in the long term?
- Do you feel I will get work quickly?
- Do I require any immediate physical changes, such as a haircut, weight loss, skin treatment or cosmetic dentistry?
- How much commission do you take?
- When and how do I get paid?
- What is/will be my hourly rate?

Remember, just because a specific agency is considered to be the best for other people does not mean that it is necessarily the best agency for you. I have actually had aspiring models argue with me that Elite is the best agency for them and they insist that I am making a mistake in not representing them. My response is, "Why would you want to be represented by an agency which does not want to represent you?" It is imperative that both the model and the agency believe in the product, understand how to market the product and agree to work together.

Over the years I have signed on quite a few models whom I have initially turned down— sometimes even twice. Timing is very important. At the time that you happen to be interviewing with an agency, it might already have a couple of models whom you resemble. The agency will protect the talent that it already has under contract and thus avoid internal competition within the same market at the same time.

If you are really determined to become a model you won't allow a few rejections to discourage you, even if you have been rejected by every agency in your market. Think about it—*why* were you rejected? Did you receive any constructive criticism that you could put into practice before trying again? Perhaps you need to lose weight, clear up bad skin or grow out an awful haircut? As I have mentioned before, an agency can

> 66 *You've got to have personality, endurance and a backbone of steel! You also have to be very tolerant because most people in this business are temperamental.*
>
> *I used to cry myself to sleep because I didn't think I was good enough. I felt better after a good cry and kept forging on.* 99
>
> Vanessa Victor
> Model

always provide reasons for rejecting someone. Many aspiring models make heartfelt promises to me, swearing that *if* I sign them with the agency, *then* they will take care of any immediate problem. I rarely listen to their promises. There are just too many other dedicated people out there for me to bet on those who haven't got their act together when they arrive for an interview. I say this so you will understand *why* some agents may reject you, *not* to scare you away from trying. You can't possibly know how each agent will respond.

Large agency, small agency, exclusive, non-exclusive, multiply listed (being represented by more than one agency)—are all controversial topics. I cannot tell you which is the best for you. Just do a lot of research, ask lots of questions (keeping notes), observe the agencies as you are interviewing to see how they operate, and then follow your instincts.

It is possible that you might make a mistake. The important thing is that you make a decision on something and take a step forward. You will continually learn if you make decisions. You are the one who must begin to take control of your new business—*you*.

> 66 *I'm always on the lookout for some special quality that makes a great face and body outstanding. Personality, style and self-confidence should shine through. If there is an element of that special quality, a good agent will develop and sell it. Once the model starts to feel that momentum, then the rush is on.* 99
>
> Huggy Ragnarsson
> Freelance scout

DAN ZAITZ

CHAPTER 2

WHEN YOU HAVE AN AGENCY

The secret of success

•

Getting to know your profession

•

Getting to know your market

•

Portfolio assembly

•

Mini-books

•

Composite assembly

•

Agency promotional book

•

Headsheet

•

Where do photographs come from?

•

Diaries

•

Wardrobe and model's bag(s)

A modeling agency can often seem like a chaotic environment to the uninitiated, but beneath the frenzy a lot of hard work is going on.

Congratulations! You've got yourself an agency and you're raring to go. At the risk of sounding like a wet blanket, I'm now going to give you a few words of caution.

Modeling is a tough business, and however sensible you are, you're bound to take some knocks. My mother always used to tell me, "When you've lost your sense of humor you've lost everything." Those words of wisdom have brought me through many difficult times as I've grown up in the fashion world. You have to maintain a great sense of humor to endure some of the nonsense that will inevitably come your way. If you laugh it off you will come through with flying colors. I tease many new interviewees that I wouldn't wish this business on anyone.

For now be warned that your life will be turned upside-down. If you are smart and keep your wits about you, you'll adjust very quickly and, hopefully, with minimal pain. It is not being cynical to say that there are nasty people in this industry—there are nasty ones outside it too. There are bound to be times when you will experience problems with such people generally.

THE SECRET OF SUCCESS

This can be quickly summed up in two words:

Sacrifice—to give up something in the short term for the sake of something better in the long term
Compete—to strive for an objective

Both these words indicate a single-mindedness which you must have to survive as a model—and sometimes they can make your life very difficult.

The model is constantly concerned with such things as diet, exercise, sleep, skin care, make-up, hair, clothes, fashion magazines, TV commercials and movies. You'll become immersed in a whole new world which you have to juggle simultaneously with your existing lifestyle. There will be endless and inevitable changes. Modeling is a very self-centered career and your family and friends may be slow to realize that your time with them will be necessarily curtailed. They'll watch you spending a lot of money that most likely won't produce an immediate return. They'll see a physical change in you as you become more educated about how to present yourself. They'll see an emotional change as you become more confident. I've seen models suffer tremendously

> *Like a professional athlete, [models] are given a talent, only in this case it's a beautiful face and a body. If you use it as a means to an end, you can create a terrific career for yourself.*
> Marjorie Graham
> Agent

because of concerned parents, jealous girlfriends and intimidated boyfriends. It takes strength of character to consider yourself and your career constantly without hurting those around you. Keeping your family and close friends abreast of your daily activities can aid the transition; this way they'll understand your involvement with some of your other concerns.

People sometimes have funny ideas about the modeling business, seeing it as one long, self-indulgent ego trip. However misconceived these ideas, they can threaten your relationships, so you'd better be prepared to decide what your sacrifices will be. It's not uncommon for models to become selfish and neurotic, but it's up to you whether you let yourself succumb to the negative aspects of the business.

What does it mean to "compete" as a model? One parallel that may help you understand the "competition" is the idea of an Olympic hopeful going after a gold medal in swimming. That swimmer spends hours training every day, as well as juggling other obligations. He or she will practice form and speed and not be distracted by developing dry skin and discolored, brittle hair, by smelling of chlorine, by missing out on social activities with family and friends, or by worrying about other swimmers who may have more experience and talent. All these things count for nothing if you have a goal you really want to achieve.

> *The kids think of rejection as a personal attack on their physical appearance, when in reality they didn't get the jobs because they just weren't right for them ... Once they establish in their own minds that they are good-looking and accept that [rejection] isn't a personal attack, they make it a lot easier on themselves.*
> Paul David Fisher
> Agent

The same single-mindedness applies to modeling. Thousands of people have preceded you in your chosen career. Many have been downright vicious and inconsiderate in reaching their goal, but you don't have to be like that, and indeed you'll get a lot further if you're not! It's always better to make friends rather than enemies.

I found a new model at a convention. The agency paid for her air fare to come to Chicago and we also paid for a hotel room for her and her father for one week. We allowed her to stay rent-free in the models' apartment. She broke the no-pets rule by getting a cat and then lied about how it got into the apartment. We advanced her money for portfolio photographs and her composite. When she got sick late one Sunday

> *Because modeling is such a selfish profession and each job can be your last, you try and learn from each job—you try and move forward—and you do tend to focus all of what you are learning into yourself. It takes a special kind of person to be able to live with not knowing where the next pay check is coming from, to accept the responsibility of never working again, and still feel very positive about yourself. Certain things, such as going to the movies with friends, become inconsequential next to working out, having a make-up lesson or going to a testing.*
>
> Andy Westerman
> Agent

night, our booker drove her to the hospital and spent the night with her because she was scared. She then returned to her home town to recuperate from her illness. We expected her to return in two weeks. Well, she returned all right! One evening I just happened to see her walking down the street arm in arm with a friend. I learned the next day that she was on an audition in Chicago through another agency. She never had the courtesy to tell us she was dissatisfied with our representation. She told people that she didn't think we believed in her look. (Well, if we didn't prove it by our attentions, what else could we have done?)

We wasted a lot of time and money because of that model, but this story is typical of many and there are hundreds more that every agent can cite. It's up to you to break the mold that this over-saturated industry has produced. If you're new and have no track record, don't take it personally if people don't bend over backwards to help you—it's because too many nasty people have tainted their enthusiasm for assisting unknown, aspiring models.

In promoting yourself (competing), people will inevitably misunderstand you and take your confidence for arrogance. What is wrong with believing in yourself? Nothing! But you must keep it all in perspective. I amaze people when I tell them that I am an excellent agent. I am! I can't balance my checking account or change a tire on a car, in fact there are lots of things I can't do, but agenting is what I do know. And I know it well! Would you want to work with an agent who didn't believe in herself? Or who couldn't make a decision or protect you and your career? How confident would you be in her representation if she were sheepish and always avoiding issues? (Recently I met up with an old high school chum, Eric and his friend. After I began updating Eric on my progress over the years, he turned to his friend and said, "Marie's not conceited, she's just convinced!" I was amused at his reaction. What do people want to hear—that I'm doing poorly and I'm not going anywhere in life? They'll never hear it from my mouth!)

You will have to work hard at establishing yourself as a competitive, considerate, confident, worthwhile product. When people tease you or question you, just laugh them off. To this day my father insists that I do not have a real job. He maintains that until I get a college degree I won't become successful. People outside this industry have a distorted perception of what really goes on. I know that modeling can be a frustrating, expensive, depressing, degrading career—on the other hand it can be educational, lucrative, uplifting and confidence-building. In order to become successful you have to maintain your own ethics and morals. Remain true to yourself, take care of yourself and the people around you, and always be professional.

> *The message you send is not always the message received, so you have to communicate carefully— check who your audience is and how you're projecting yourself. In part, we know who we are based upon feedback from other people. It works in a loop. We have to project an image. People respond to us based upon what they think they see—perhaps it's confidence, the way we dress, or the way we walk. Our own self-concept develops from other people's reactions to us.*
>
> Donna Surges-Tatum
> Professor of Communications
> Roosevelt University

GETTING TO KNOW YOUR PROFESSION

A model is a product, just like any other product that is being sold. The main difference is that the model is a human being, and as such is capable of emotions which can sometimes interfere with the sale. It is crucial that you understand the industry in order to learn how to separate the emotional part of yourself from the product part. I have a simple analogy that might lend insight to this difficult process.

Do you brush your teeth? What brand of toothpaste do you use? How long have you been using that brand? Chances are you have either used the same brand for years or you change brands very quickly. Similarly, photographers and clients might use the same models for years or they might change very quickly.

It is very difficult to know what each client's habits are and how to handle them. Aim to be consistent in your behavior and approach at each meeting, keeping in mind the intention of selling the product. Modeling is a business, just like any other. The glamor and excitement of the business do not mean that you should be any less professional in your approach.

25

How did you hear about your particular brand(s) of toothpaste? Word of mouth, television commercials, magazine advertisements, billboards? All these sources and more are called advertising. No matter what the source, if the product is being talked about or seen, it's being advertised. It is imperative that you advertise your product, too. You advertise yourself through word of mouth, through photographers, make-up artists, hairdressers and stylists, through your portfolio and composite, and through your print bookings (published photographs). These are all components of your advertising campaign. A modeling agency acts as your advertising agency and it is essential to have one before going any further. You should not spend any more on your advertising campaign until you have a strategy determining how you will design, package and advertise yourself. It is the agent's responsibility to assess the product (you) and to speculate on your marketability in their market and others. Such assessments are based upon years of experience in working with models and clients, and traveling around the world doing research.

The market is the most important factor in a successful career. A model could make a lot of money shooting catalogue in Hamburg, Germany, then go to New York and possibly never work in catalogue. To be successful, you must place your product in the market(s) most likely to purchase you. (Chances are that you won't sell many Black hair products in a predominantly White neighborhood store and vice-versa. The strategy would be to sell minority products in areas where the minorities live.) Be sure to do your research before going into any market; the ways of doing this are more fully described on page 28.

> 66 *I'm very conscious of my appearance—to me it's all part of the business. It's packaging—just like any other product. One tip I'd give to new models is that personality and how you present yourself are the basis of how the client will interact with you.* 99
>
> Michael Ramion
> Model

Reputation

Do you know people who, no matter what they say they'll do, just never do it? Even as they are saying the words you are sure they'll never follow through, so eventually you never take them seriously. Can you honestly claim you are not one of these people? Do *you* always do what you say you are going to do?

Do you know people who, no matter when you speak to them, are always unhappy and have a negative attitude? They just never have anything

> 66 *You must realize that there are hundreds of kids who can do the same job as you. The clients want something a little more special than someone to fill the job. They are looking for a personality and attitude of professionalism that they can work with. Everyone wants to have a pleasant day; make the clients' job easy so they can leave the shoot smiling.* 99
>
> Allan Boyd
> Model

pleasant or nice to say? It's so depressing that you may even want to go in another direction when you see them coming! Do you come across in a negative way?

Do you know people who, no matter when you speak to them, are always happy and have a positive attitude? Do they always have something nice to say and uplift you no matter what your mood? You'll probably even go out of your way just to say hello to such people if they're coming in your direction! Do *you* come across in a positive way?

The thoughts people have about you could be considered your reputation. All products have reputations, and a model's is closely linked to attitude; sometimes they are bad and sometimes they are good. Be sure you develop an enthusiastic, dependable, positive reputation early in your career. That reputation will follow you throughout life.

Imagine yourself as a tube of toothpaste on a store shelf. You have to design your package to compete against other brands, both established and new. What makes your product so special and different? Why should the customer select your product instead of another one? What do you have to offer that someone else does not? Yes, this may sound silly, but if you now understand the parallel, you have come a long way in understanding your profession and making your career more successful.

> 66 *The secret of success is not simply being beautiful – attitude, initiative, determination and a fun personality are other important elements.* 99
>
> Cela Wise
> Model and actress

Whether you're new to the modeling business, or an old hand, it's important to keep up with trends in fashion photography. The best way to do this is to subscribe to a wide variety of magazines — especially Vogue and Elle.

GETTING TO KNOW YOUR MARKET

The market is the city and the type of clients there. If you are just beginning your career as a model, you may not know a lot about your market. All the more reason to research your city well. If you're planning on going into a new market or city, you must ask lots of questions and read as much about that area as you can. Ask where the work is, where you fit in and what percentage of the market your "look" fills. If there is not a high demand for you, you might consider moving to another market. Chapters 5 and 6 discuss the different "looks" and "markets" more extensively.

Your agent could well be your main source of reference, but do phrase your questions precisely or you may get misleading answers. For example, some agents rarely travel outside the country in which they operate, so they do not know the way a foreign market works. However, this might not deter them from giving you fifth-hand information which could be riddled with inaccuracies.

To avoid this sort of problem, always ask direct questions, such as: Have you been to Milan? What sort of look do they like? And make sure you get direct answers. If in any doubt, ask fellow models who have done what you want to do for the benefit of their experience. Telephone agencies in the particular market you're going to and ask for their advice (some provide fact sheets). Note that agencies throughout the world speak English and most will be happy to pass on a few local hints. For general information about foreign markets (climate, customs and so on), contact the country's tourist office for free literature. At the very least, visit your local reference library. If you end up in a totally alien environment, like Japan, you'll be thankful to have done your research thoroughly.

Over the years I have seen many models who have been improperly marketed. As a result, I have learned daily lessons on how to prevent the models I deal with from making the same mistakes. The secret is to develop your own understanding of the market and to realize the importance of marketing yourself within the market you wish to work.

A good professional model can work in just about any market. However, as a new model it would be wise for you to start your career in a market with a high demand for your look. Keep in mind that each time you change markets your agent will change your portfolio and composite to adapt your look for that specific market.

PORTFOLIO ASSEMBLY

We have already established that your portfolio is one of the key components of your advertising campaign. Now you need to know how to put it together. Every agent will address this area differently. However, I am sure we would all agree that the photos inside your book should be only the best you can provide at that time in your career. I have interviewed thousands of models over the years, many of whom believe that *any* photo is better than none. I disagree totally! Remember, you are competing with thousands of models around the world, so you should only show photos that make you look terrific. Note too, that it is a mistake to show contact sheets, as you probably do not look perfect in every shot.

It does not matter whether you have more black and white photos than color; great pictures are great pictures, regardless of their color. Some agents might suggest that you shoot more black and white than color because it is less expensive. (In the UK agents always want to see some black and white photos in a portfolio—even when the

A portfolio should tell a story which holds the viewer's interest from beginning to end.
1 The opening page should be bold, showing a shot of the model looking terrific. This is often the main shot used on the comp-card.
2 Focusing on the hands, feet and complexion, this spread shows that the model is suitable for part modeling.
3 This editorial spread shows the proportions of the model's body and that she has worked successfully in Japan.
4 In a swimsuit, the viewer can see that the model is in good shape. The left-hand page also shows her suitability for part modeling.
5 Revealing bikini shots show that the model is suitable for modeling lingerie.
6 This spread shows the model wearing light, casual clothing. It also shows that she can interact well with other models.
7 The clothes are bright and relaxed in this spread, and the setting is distinctly summery.
8 A young, informal spread, this is impressive because it's the front cover of a large circulation magazine.
9 In winter-time it's a good idea to finish your "story" wearing appropriate clothing — coats, sweaters, hats and so on.
10 The final page in the portfolio has a more "adult," sophisticated shot in black and white which shows the model's versatility.

> " *Don't arrive unannounced. Have your agency contact another agency in the city that you wish to visit. Be sure to send comps in advance so that they can promote you before you arrive. Your agency can do the groundwork by calling for you in advance to inquire about the market, but then it's your task to get out and see the clients once you arrive.* "
>
> Paul Wadina
> Model

1   MARK ASH

2   TED DAYTON

3   JACKIE WINTER

4   JACKIE WINTER   KEN CHERNETH

5   JEAN-PAUL PECACHE   RYAN ROBINSON

6   KEN CHERNETH

7

8   TEKE

9   JAIME LOPEZ   COLIN BOOKER

10   COLIN BOOKER

1 DOUGLAS KEEVE

2 GRANT MATHEWS   GRAM SHEARER

3 ALDO FALLAI

4 MONTY COLES   GRANT MATHEWS

5 DOUGLAS KEEVE

6 GIOVANNI GASTEL

7 GIOVANNI GASTEL

8 EAMONN J. McCABE   CLAUS WICKRATH

9 DOUGLAS KEEVE

10 BOB GOTHARD

30

model is experienced.) Some companies in large markets can print color quickly and cheaply. You can express your slides to them by courier and have your color prints returned in a few days. Again, you should rely on your agency for proper direction in all these areas.

I feel that your portfolio should "read" just like any other book: it should have a terrific beginning, a strong middle and a sensational ending. Remember, you should have people wanting to turn the pages with curiosity! Each page should satisfy that curiosity. It should display your strengths to potential clients and show what you are capable of selling, be it clothes, cars or cosmetics.

In the beginning it is very difficult to provide each client with photos they can identify with. Don't get frustrated—it will all come in good time. I have already mentioned the importance of patience. If you don't have any now, you'd better find some. The development of a portfolio can be a very expensive, long and arduous process, but well worth it.

The types of photo you should shoot depend on what you have to sell and your market. (Some experienced models will have different books for different markets.) In the early days heed your agent's advice and use your common sense. If you have a great body, perhaps you'll shoot a lot of body shots. If you have excellent skin and hair, shoot a lot of beauty shots. If your legs are terrific, shoot a few leg shots. The idea is to advertise what you have to offer the clients, concentrating on your best features. If your body is not that

1 *The opening page of this model's portfolio has a simple but striking photo.*
2 *An outdoor, autumnal spread with some "action" shots.*
3 *These tailored casual clothes convey a more up-market image.*
4 *The preppy look, with patterned sweater and tweed jacket. Note how the longer hair and prop spectacles markedly change the model's appearance. The right-hand photo also shows his ability to interact well with other models.*
5 *This "action" spread is an interesting change of pace. It shows the model looking energetic and rugged, and working efficiently with another model.*
6 *These shots of "working" clothes follow on well from the previous spread of tailored clothes.*
7 *A jeans shot is a must — it shows the model looking good in casual wear.*
8 *This is a smart casual spread which shows the proportions of the model's body.*
9 *An atmospheric outdoor shot showing the model in very casual summer clothes.*
10 *The portfolio closes with another simple but strong image. This shows clearly that it is better to have a good image alone rather than next to a conflicting one.*

> *Clients like to see photos in a portfolio that they can identify with to reinforce their decision to book that model. Their image has to be reflected in that model. I will often edit a book for a specific client so that they only see the images they see in themselves. It's better to have a few appropriate images than a lot that may distract or confuse the client.*
>
> John David
> Agent

competitive yet, do not shoot body shots. If your skin and hair are not in excellent condition, you'd better start getting them there; do not shoot beauty shots until you are ready!

It is very important to be versatile. However, do not be so extreme and inconsistent that you confuse the client. Models often show themselves so completely differently that a client cannot get a fix on how they will look for their photo session. You must always show yourself in a relatively similar way. Until you are experienced and really understand yourself my best advice is to keep things straightforward—the make-up and hair, soft; lighting, simple; the clothes and mood, uncomplicated.

The total number of photos that you should use from each photo session depends primarily on the art direction. For an editorial spread, you might use as many as five photos, say, one large and four small. The large one could be displayed on one side of the spread and the four smaller photos opposite. If you have only one terrific photo, I would prefer to see it alone rather than displayed with a photo that clashes. For example, it would be a mistake to display a bathing suit shot next to a fur coat.

If possible, also try to include photos of you interacting with other models. This will show catalogue clients that you can work with others in a compatible way. However, do not include such a photo if you are not looking your best. If another model is the focus of the photo, your agent will decide if it is wise to show you next to competition.

> *A portfolio is one of the two most powerful tools that a model can have (your comp being the other one). Your portfolio is an extension and elaboration of your comp. Start simple: learn from your agent and clients about your photos. You'll learn and develop as you become more experienced.*
>
> George Weeks
> Model

At the beginning of your fashion modeling career your portfolio should include:

- At least two head shots with two different expressions (one smiling and one serious, or one in the studio and one out of doors).

- At least two fashion shots (one casual and one a little more formal). If you move well, you might like to include an action shot.

- At least one full-length shot showing the proportions of your body (feet to knees, knees to thighs, thighs to waist, waist to shoulders, shoulders to the top of your head). You could wear a bathing suit, leotard or lingerie, depending on what makes you comfortable and is the most flattering to your figure.

I have a theory that I normally follow when I arrange a portfolio. I begin with fall/winter and go into spring/summer seasons if I'm arranging the book during the colder months, and vice versa if I'm doing it during warmer weather. This means that models either start with lots of clothes and slowly take them off, or start in bathing suits and lingerie and slowly add more clothes until wearing heavy sweaters and coats.

You can also include photos of yourself participating in sports or other activities towards the end. You may be an equestrian, so include a photo of you jumping. If you are a terrific skier, include a photo of you on the slopes. If you have a nice photo of you on the runway, include that too. The idea is to advertise what you have to sell. If your portfolio doesn't win you one job, it may open up a conversation that could eventually lead you into another one.

If you have a particular skill, such as swimming, horseback-riding or rock-climbing, it is a good idea to include a shot of you in action.

MICHAEL THOMPSON

FAMOUS BARR

VICTOR SKREBNESKI

These two spreads are a clear example of how a model can be skilfully marketed. The serious, almost solemn shots (**top**) convey quite a different mood from those below. Although he is not the sole focus of the group shots, he is shown to advantage, and his versatility is clearly conveyed to the viewer.

Portfolio size

The actual portfolio can be various sizes these days, but generally they are getting smaller; this makes them easier to carry around, as well as to flip through. The usual US size for a big book is 9 x 12½in. You will eventually need three mini-books in addition to your big book. Some agencies have their own books with their logos printed on them. You don't have to have one of these, but it can help to advertise yourself. Remember, your book protects your photos and its appearance is a reflection of you. If the plastic pages inside become scratched and worn-looking, replace them. Your book should always look immaculate and professional. You can choose various types: zippered, handled, shoulder-strapped or plain—it is up to you, but keep it looking like a book and make sure it's simple to open. You can buy your book through your agency or at an art supply store.

Normally you should have only your plastic pages, possibly a sleeve of your slides, and your comps inside your books. It is so irritating to be handed a book and out fall all sorts of distractions—old photos, shopping lists, daily diary ... Your book is your advertising campaign, so keep it clean and beautifully presented.

MINI-BOOKS

Mini-books are portfolios measuring 5 x 7in. They usually have ten pages, allowing you to display 20 single photos. You may wonder why a smaller version of your big book is necessary. The reasons are endless: what if you lose your big book or it is stolen? What if you need your big book for go-sees in your city and you have three clients all wanting your book overnight? The agency can send these mini-books by overnight courier directly to the clients. This way you'll have a better chance of getting work out of town. Clients aren't too keen on booking models from their composite cards alone. If they can't see you in person, the mini-book will represent you well in your absence. It also pays to keep a mini-book in your model's bag. That way if you go into a booking and the client has not seen your portfolio you can immediately pull out your mini-book.

Do not get a mini-book until you are 6–8 months into your career. This way you're more likely to have a "timeless" set of pictures; at the very least they'll last for a year. Eventually you should have a mini-book for each market you work in.

My agency has been using Bookitt in Dallas, Texas, for all its portfolio needs. We call the owners the Bookitt Boys. If you send them your pictures by overnight courier, they'll return your original pictures within two working days. You'll receive your three mini portfolios with the three sets of reduced photos within one week.

A mini-book is an exact duplicate of your portfolio, but only a quarter of the size — ideal for carrying around in your model's bag and for sending to prospective clients if your big book is "out."

MIKE DONNALLY

COMPOSITE ASSEMBLY

Your composite is another key component in your advertising campaign. Your comp-card is your business card. It communicates who you are, your body's statistics, a sampling of your capabilities in front of the camera and your agency's logo with the name, address and phone number. How this information is arranged is decided by you and your agent—and the design possibilities are infinite. Modeling is a very creative industry, so make sure your card looks slick and professional, reflecting well on you and your agency.

Your best photos should be selected for your comp-card. This might mean you end up with only three photos on your card, but don't worry. If they sell you in an honest way, the card will do its job. Even with these "introductory" cards, the presentation has to be beautiful and professional, regardless of the quantity and color of the photos. Every model has to start somewhere. If you're new, the industry does not expect you to have an expensive, color, tri-fold comp. You have to develop at your own pace.

At the beginning of your fashion modeling career, your card will most likely be a standard 8 x 5½in in black and white. Quite apart from the fact that color is more expensive and takes longer to print, I really don't feel it's necessary, so don't waste your money. Give yourself time to learn your trade and develop your ability to move and project your personality on camera; you will be much better six months into your career. Please do not use color photos on your comp until you are certain they will be current for at least a year and you have the time and money to invest in color. It can't be said too often: good photos are good photos, regardless of their color.

The kind of photos you use depends upon you and your market. What do you have to sell? How can you compete? Are you in a catalogue or editorial market? (Chapter 5 deals with these considerations in more detail.) Remember, common sense is crucial in putting together a good comp-card. Keep your advertising campaign in your mind constantly. Your composite is an extension of you and the agency—be sure that it sells you both.

A good comp-card is a vital part of a model's advertising campaign. Always use your best photos and don't invest in color until you have acquired some "timeless" shots.

Introducing....

KAREN PARKS

Wilger

PHOTO COLLAGE DAVID FLEISHMAN

AGENCY PROMOTIONAL BOOK

Despite its name, this is another part of *your* advertising campaign. Every agency has a promotional piece of some kind. The bigger agencies produce "books," which are rather like collections of comp-cards. All the models the agency represents are featured in the book, and the photos are accompanied by their statistics and union standings.

As with all the other parts of a model's advertising campaign, the cost of being featured in the book is borne by the model. However, the benefits to be gained from inclusion are priceless. Clients, agencies and photographers at home and around the world "shop" for models from these books, so it is possible to get overseas bookings with minimal effort. The books also continue to promote you in your absence from a particular market, and are much harder to mislay than loose comp-cards.

Models are responsible for making their book submissions promptly. It is a serious matter to be late, as hold-ups can jeopardize the production of the book for everyone. Try not to be guilty of this.

HEADSHEET

Every agency produces a poster with small head shots of each of the models it represents. This headsheet is sent out to photographers and all potential clients as a quick reference. New models are added to the headsheet once they have suitable photos—usually within three months of starting with an agency.

STANDARD RELEASE FORM

Standard release form for signature by models
issued by the Association of Fashion, Advertising and Editorial
Photographers, Association of Model Agents and the Institute of
Practitioners in Advertising

NAME OF PHOTOGRAPHER _____
NAME OF 'ADVERTISING AGENCY CLIENT _____

PRODUCT, SERVICE OR PURPOSE _____

NEGATIVE SERIES NO. _____ ORDER NO. _____ DATE _____

In consideration of the sum of £...... and any other sums which may become due to me under the above Associations' current 'Terms, conditions and standards for the engagement of professional models in still photography", and conditionally upon due payment of the aforesaid sums and the undertaking of the 'Advertising Agency Client Photographer given below, I permit the 'Advertising Agency Client Photographer and its licensees or assignees to use the photograph(s) referred to above and or drawings therefrom and any other reproductions or adaptations thereof either complete or in part, alone or in conjunction with any wording and. or drawings solely and exclusively for:

* **EDITORIAL**
* **EXPERIMENTAL**
* **PR**
* **PRESS ADVERTISING**
* **POSTER ADVERTISING** (4 sheet upwards)
* **DISPLAY MATERIAL AND POSTERS** (under 4 sheet)
* **PACKAGING**
in relation to the above product, service or purpose
* **IN THE UNITED KINGDOM**
* **IN EUROPE**
* **WORLDWIDE**

         * MODEL MUST DELETE IF NOT APPLICABLE

I understand that such copyright material shall be deemed to represent an imaginary person unless agreed, in writing, by my agent or myself.
I understand that I do not own the copyright of the photograph(s).

'I am over 18 years of age.

NAME (in capitals) _____
SIGNATURE OF MODEL _____
ADDRESS AGENT _____
DATE _____ WITNESS _____

Models who are under 18 years of age must produce evidence of consent by their parent or guardian.

In accepting the above release the 'Advertising Agency/Client/Photographer undertakes that the copyright material shall only be used in accordance with the terms of the release.

* MODEL MUST DELETE IF NOT APPLICABLE

Above *After photo shoots, it is normal practice for the models to sign a "release form," which gives the photographer/client formal permission to use the photographs in specified markets. (In the US, a smaller form called a "voucher" is sometimes used instead.) Never sign any form without first speaking to your agent about what markets you should agree to—you might lose out on fees.*

Below *and right A headsheet is a poster showing small pictures of each of the models an agency represents.*

Elite

Elite
Chicago
Jane Stewart
John Casablancas

212 West Superior Street
Suite 406
Chicago, Illinois
60610
Tel: (312) 943-3226
T.V. (312) 943-3131
Telex: 4330398
Fax (312) 943-2590

Alison Alberts · Lisa Anderson · Aria · Deborah Armstrong · Carina Asuncion · Arlene Baxter · Beth Behrends · Kim Davis

Kathryn Bishop · Stephanie Averill · Susan Brown · Leslie Caldwell · Sylvia Carroll · Diana Chambers · Trina Chambers · Pamela Chennells

Karen Collmer · Linda Cook · Lisa Coolidge · Rita Craig · Cindy Crawford · Tara Danette · Lisa Delich · Suzanne Duncan

Mari Fox · Sandra Freeman · Michelle Ganeles · Carol Gardner · Erin Gastineau · Tiffany Green · Amy Harris · Michelle Haupert

Janelle Hensley · Kristin Holland · Tera Johnson · Laura Justice · Lynn Kempton · Kelly Killoren · Carole Kurzin · Jennifer Kusner

Amy Lada · Tracy Lambert · Melanie Lawrence · Anna Lee · Mei-Li · Dawn Marie · Traci Martinson · Michele Meiché

Candy Middleton · Cynthia Moore · Lizbeth Mustari · Tara Mys · Dana Nemer · Kristen Noel · Amy Owen · Karen Parks

Dana Patrick · Pia · Victoria Prouty · Katrina Rae · Tanya Rhodes · Linda Ryan · Jane Sanguinetti · Ellen Sturman

Pam Skaggs · Monique St. Claire · Amy Marie Vollmer · Cindy Waite · Loretta Wilger · Madeline Williams · Michele Williams · Tasha

WHERE DO PHOTOGRAPHS COME FROM?

If you're a new model and have no photos, how do you go about getting them?

In the US the normal method of acquiring photos is through "testing." Originally this meant that a photographer would have an idea for a shoot and ask a model to collaborate with him on it at his expense. Now, however, a model is just as likely to initiate the idea and hire a photographer (plus make-up artist and stylist) to shoot at her expense. In my opinion, this is good news: the model is not hanging around waiting for a photographer to do her a "favor;" she is in more active control of the test and her financial involvement usually focuses the attention of all concerned, resulting in better photos.

Your agent will advise you how to go about setting up a test and who to approach. In your role as "client," you can pick and choose who to work with, so make sure you view various photographers' books and find someone in whom you have confidence.

At the beginning of a model's career, I discourage her from shooting her entire book with one photographer. I generally recommend shooting with two photographers (of my choice) as they will undoubtedly see the model differently. I make the recommendations based on budget and talent—unlike some agents who only recommend those from whom they get kickbacks. Testing is a big expense, but remember, you are investing in yourself and you can't expect to work until you have some photos in your portfolio. After you have seen a photographer, always tell your agent what fee has been quoted—this will prevent the photographer from quoting a higher fee than that agreed with your agent.

Testing is a great opportunity to extend yourself and take a few risks, especially if you are in a catalogue market with no editorial: you don't have the pressures and restrictions of a booking. Develop at your own pace and never compare yourself with anyone else. (I know of a set of twins where one twin works more than the other. Why? There could be several reasons: personality and professionalism have a lot to do with it, as do the abilities to move and project different emotions. The market is also a consideration. How many times can a market book their "look?")

Sometimes a model may be approached to do a test by other beginners in the modeling business—

A team of new talent (aspiring photographer, make-up artist, clothing stylist and model) may pool their abilities to set up a shoot and each will use the resulting photos in their portfolios. (Note the model's rolled-up trousers and tennis shoes, which will not be part of the shot.) Inset *The finished photograph.*

photo assistants, or new hairdressers, make-up artists and stylists. Costs may be shared and all will get the benefit of good photos to add to their portfolios. If you are not a complete beginner, you may not have to contribute anything to the costs. Have a thorough discussion about financial responsibility before any testing takes place and make sure that every member of the team has a clear understanding of the arrangements. As you become a better business person, you will learn how to be your own art director and negotiate the finances without offending your peers.

> 66 *Some established photographers test at no cost to the model. These tests are specifically for the photographer. However, sometimes a photographer will favor a model and assist them on portfolio development at the photographer's expense.* 99

> Richard Noiret
> Photographer

If you are to get maximum value from your tests, preparation is necessary. Dancing and acting classes can help you develop the ability to move and emote, but simply practicing these things in front of a mirror is also beneficial. Photographers frequently complain that models "jerk" from one position to another on set. To train yourself out of this, stand in front of a full-length mirror wearing a swimsuit or leotard, and move slowly from one position to another, like a dancer. For head shots move close into the mirror and rehearse various emotions. Watch your face and remember the thoughts it takes to bring out those emotions so you can summon them up again in shoots whenever necessary. (Don't worry about feeling foolish—it's all valuable to your career.)

In catalogue shoots, when the deadline is always pressing and photos have to be taken very quickly, clients do not want the photographer's time to be used up in getting models to pose correctly. If you develop the skill of moving well, and thus complement the product, you'll be in great demand!

In any photo session it is essential to understand what is required. You must "become" the photo and direct every ounce of your energy toward the camera. No matter what your mood, you must always give your best and leave any unhappy feelings outside the studio. If you are not "into" a photo, it will probably "read" onto the film—even if the rest of the team has done a first-rate job. *You* are the key to the success of a photo.

A testing is just as important as a booking: it should be taken just as seriously and handled just as professionally. Plan ahead, arrive on time and have everything you need to ensure success.

DIARIES

Your daily diary (date book) is also called your "industry bible," and it is vital to have a good one. Many agencies produce their own and include lots of useful information and addresses relevant to the modeling world. If you prefer to put together your own "bible," a Filofax is ideal as it has masses of pockets and can expand to fit your needs. The most important thing is that you have enough room to write on each page. (This demonstrates the power of positive thinking: you'll need lots of room to write down all the things you'll be doing!)

These diaries generally measure 6 x 7in and have a page a day. You should write every daily detail inside—in ink if definite, in pencil if provisional; this is all part of becoming organized

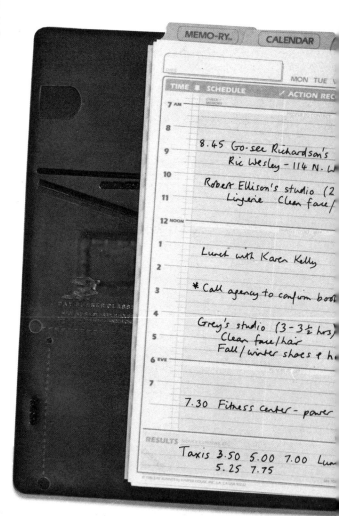

and professional and the benefits are unlimited. For a start, it will remind you of your bookings and perhaps a note of how the client wants you to look—elegant, good nails, swimsuit, or whatever. It will also provide a valuable record for such things as audits: you can always look back in your diary to check queries about receipts, payments and hours worked. If your agent is organizing an audition, always check the booking date to make sure that you don't have a conflicting engagement. At your bookings you should write down the name of everyone you meet—that way you'll always have a record of your interactions and build up a network of contacts. If your agency's book-keeping department has any questions about a past booking, just look it up in your date book. Keep your daily diary close by and commit nothing to memory—write everything down.

> ❝ *To me, my daily diary is invaluable. My schedule is so hectic that I need to have everything written down. It's extremely important for looking back on such things as taxes, miles driven, where you went, who you were with, the rates, etc.* ❞
>
> Tracy Lambert
> Model

> ❝ *One tip I have for models is to write down the names and positions of each person they meet at a shoot. The clients will be impressed that they remember their names when they return.* ❞
>
> Allan Boyd
> Model

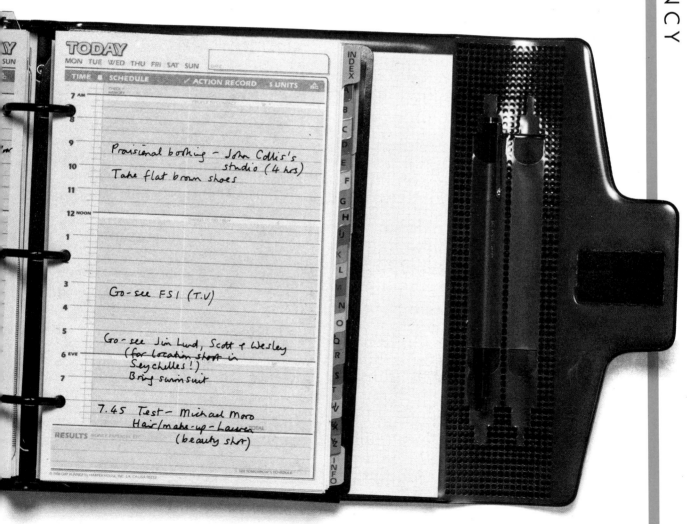

WARDROBE AND MODEL'S BAG(S)

Your wardrobe is the packaging of your product. Be sure that your package always looks fresh and planned. When you look at yourself before leaving home ask yourself if your outfit is consistent with your advertising scheme. Ask your agent what is appropriate for the market. Each market has its own requirements. In places like Dallas, Texas, and St Louis, Missouri, they prefer models to dress up and use a lot of make-up. However, in places like London or New York models tend to dress down, wearing minimal accessories and make-up. Use your common sense. Everyone has his or her own style. Don't imitate others if it's not *you*. If you're not comfortable with your clothes, it will be difficult to sell yourself at go-sees.

Model's bags carry the tools of your trade and these vary from market to market. Ask your agent what is appropriate for your market. With time and experience, a model will learn what to carry and be able to anticipate what clients will like. For now, the basic requirements are:

WOMEN: DAILY BAG
- Bras (various styles: beige, white and black)
- Panties (various styles: beige, white and black)
- Body stocking (to match your skin-color)
- Slips (various styles: beige, white and black)
- Pantyhose (sandalfoot: flesh-colored and black)
- Dress shields
- Shoes (high-heels and flats: black, white, beige)
- Hair and make-up bags (see Chapter 3)
- Nail-care bag (emery boards, clippers, buffer, polish)
- Jewelry selection
- Hygiene necessities (tampons, deodorant, razor)
- Tube top (any color)

Eventual requirements for catalogue work
- Boots
- Shoes (white sneakers, loafers, topsiders, various flats and heels)
- Socks (various colors and styles)
- Skirts (various colors and seasonal fabrics)
- Pants (various colors and seasonal fabrics)
- Blouses (various colors and fabrics: casual and dressy styles)
- Accessories (scarves, headbands, hats, gloves, sunglasses, prop spectacles, belts, jewelry)

A client may ask for additional items before a shoot, but if a model is unable to supply them, he or she should notify the client. The company may offer to supply them, or instruct the model to buy them.

You do not need to take your model's bag to go-sees, but the following basic requirements are necessary:
- Bra and panties (beige)
- Pantyhose (flesh-colored and black)
- Shoes (flat and high-heeled)
- Clean hands and nails (polish must be unchipped)

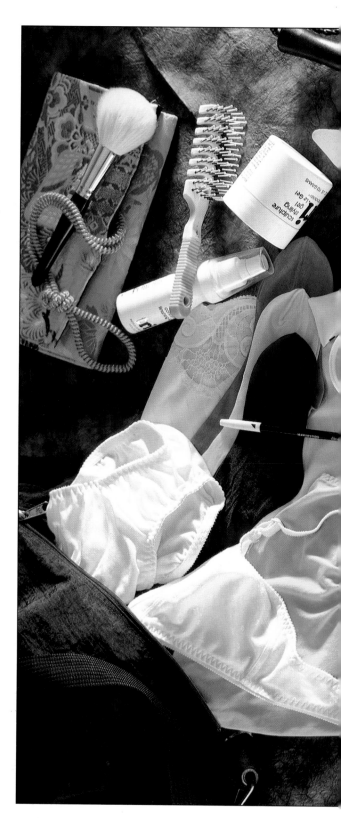

> *To me, the fact that models bring their model's bag is just as important as their looks. If they haven't brought anything to assist the shoot, I consider that a knock against them.*
>
> Laura O'Connor
> Freelance stylist

DAN ZAITZ

Model's bag for women *Below* is a selection of the items you should always carry in your bag. Although it looks like a huge amount, it fits easily into a medium-sized bag (see above) and is not inconveniently heavy.

MICHAEL ROBERTS

MEN: DAILY BAG

- Underwear (white and flesh-colored briefs, jock strap and liners)
- Socks (various colors and styles)
- Shoes (white sneakers, basic black shoes)
- Pants (various colors and seasonal fabrics)
- Make-up (base and powder to match your skin tone)
- Hair products (spray, gel, brush, comb, etc.)
- Hygiene necessities (deodorant, eye drops, contact lens solutions, razors, etc.)

Eventual requirements for catalogue work

- Shoes (white sneakers, running shoes, black and brown dress shoes, black and brown casual shoes, cowboy boots, sandals, topsiders)
- Shirts (dress shirts, sports shirts, casual shirts in a variety of colors)
- Pants (various colors and fabrics, including denim)
- Swimwear (boxer-style shorts and plain color briefs)
- Accessories (prop spectacles, watch, gold band, etc.)

Model's bag for men *Male models need to carry fewer items than women, especially in the cosmetics line, but they must have a reasonable range of accessories. The selection of equipment shown here would probably be carried by an established model.*

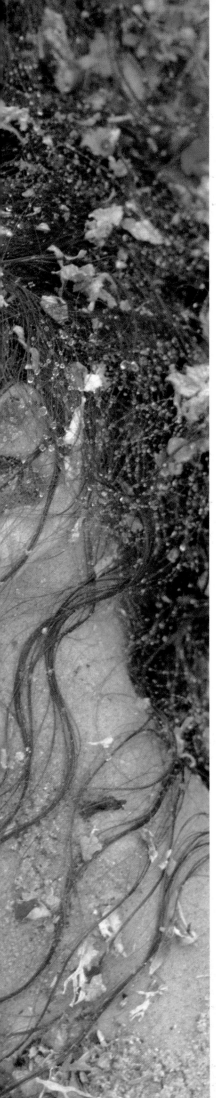

CHAPTER 3

BEAUTY

Skin care
•
Make-up
•
Hair
•
The body beautiful

Make-up has two main functions: camouflage and enhancement. A clear, glowing skin is an essential base, but once you have that you can create a face for any occasion.

As a modeling agent dealing constantly with a variety of models, I know how vital a good beauty care regime is in self-presentation. That is why I invited two experts in these fields to collaborate with me in writing this chapter: Darcy McGrath on skin care and make-up, and Judith Gold on hair. I chose them because I have worked extensively with both and they have experience in the salon *and* in the international photo and film industries. Their expertise is crucial to ensure that you get the most current and informed advice. There are many talented professionals who could have written this chapter with me; I simply chose those whose work I know and trust.

This chapter also touches on manicures, pedicures, dental work, personal hygiene and plastic surgery—important topics in a professional modeling career. However, I stress that these subjects are only touched on here, as this is *not* a beauty book. If you want to read more, there are many other books that cover these topics in detail.

SKIN CARE
by Darcy McGrath

Good skin is an essential asset to any model, and the information given here applies equally to men and women. A disciplined approach to skin care and make-up is vital if you are to weather the barrage of cosmetics, creams, lotions and paints that your face will be subjected to as a professional model. Remember, it is not only what you use in topical application, but what you eat and drink, how many cigarettes you smoke, and the amount of fresh air and exercise you get that contribute to the state of your skin. Cosmetics should only be applied to a scrupulously clean skin, but first you must assess your skin and its needs. There are several skin types and each requires a personalized regime of cleansing, toning, moisturizing and protecting.

Oily/blemished skin

With this skin-type you can feel like a dog chasing its tail. A pimply adolescence dominated by forbidden foods, harsh cleansers and anti-acne creams can create a roller-coaster effect on a skin-care cycle already screaming for balance. I find that alternating gel and milk cleansers gives great relief to an oily skin with dry patches, which suffers from underlying acne, or maybe just occasional "breakouts." The commonly used clay or other hardening masks suffocate the oxygen flow to the outer layer of skin, leaving it pink and healthier-looking once rinsed off thoroughly. Although masking is a good idea to remove dry, dead skin cells, over-frequent use of masks can cause dryness. Steaming has a relaxing effect, but can also cause irritation and possible breakouts, depending on the sensitivity of the problem.

All these skin care remedies have their place, but must be used in moderation. Over-use of buff puffs, complexion brushes, loofahs, facial scrubs and cleansing grains, can actually stimulate faster oil production, dryness and pimples. If you do use these things, I suggest you avoid using them on a daily basis. Non-abrasive exfoliators designed to remove dry skin cells from oily skin may be safely used two or three times a week, followed by your normal cleansing routine. A non-comedogenic (non-clogging) moisturizer in a gel base helps to heal the skin, as well as to protect it after cleansing. Note that detergent soaps, rubbing alcohol, excessive exposure to the sun and waterproof sunblock can also stimulate acne.

No matter how oily your skin, beware over-cleansing: it can leave the skin feeling dehydrated and looking lifeless.

If you suffer from acne or regular breakouts and are combining over-the-counter products, such as benzoyl peroxide, drying cleansers, soaps and astringents, you are probably seeing the consequent drying effects on your skin. If your breakout is monthly or occasional, only use these products on the affected area, *not* on the entire face and *never* near the eyes. If you suffer frequent breakouts and are concerned about scarring, consult a dermatologist who knows about cosmetics and will investigate your problem before administering topical or internal medicine. It has been my experience that antibiotics result in a temporary rather than a lifetime cure, and in my opinion, it is not a good idea to rely on internal medication to achieve skin balance.

Oily skin

If your skin is oily but blemish-free, try cleansing morning and evening (more often, if absolutely necessary) with gels or milk products. Follow this with a very low alcohol-content toner to remove

The skin must be thoroughly cleansed before applying a mask or make-up.

STEPHEN WOLTER

dead skin cells and any cleanser residue. Astringents with a very high alcohol content can stimulate oil glands and accelerate the speed with which their secretions rise to the surface. A non-comedogenic (gel-based) moisturizer can be safely used by this skin-type (see *Oily/blemished skin*). Masking twice a week with clay or mud masks is essential. Don't forget to use a lightweight eye cream before masking and at night. When exposed to the sun, use a non-waterproof sunblock with a protection factor of at least 19.

Dry skin

I suggest the use of a mild cleanser for dry skin—definitely no scrubs, buff puffs, loofahs or harsh soaps. Milk or cream cleansers are best, not only for removing make-up, but for ritual cleansing as well. Alcohol-free toners (not astringents) should follow all cleansings; they will remove excess cleanser and restore a smooth tone to the skin. I find this skin-type demands moisturizer all the time, and therefore prefer to use a lightweight, deep-penetrating, water-based moisturizer first, followed by a protective, heavier

Masking helps to cleanse, balance and moisturize the skin, so it's a good practice for all skin-types.

moisturizer. Night creams are essential—don't forget your neck and bust area—but use them with a light hand. Eye cream is especially important but don't apply it too close to the lids at night as it can cause puffiness.

If dryness or flaking appears, hydrating masks and gentle, cream-based exfoliators should be used once or twice a week. A high protection factor sunblock (30) will also help to protect the skin from the sun's drying rays, so incorporate it into your skin-care regime if you live or work in a sunny climate.

Dehydration can also occur from central heating and air conditioning, extreme hot or cold climates, flying, unsuitable cleansers, alcohol and coffee consumption, certain prescribed medicines and excessive tanning, so beware all these things.

Sensitive skin

This skin-type is frequently related to dry skin. It may react badly to certain cosmetics, metals, foods, beverages and alcohol-based skin-care products. Common signs of sensitive skin may be rashes, ruddiness, dryness and broken surface capillaries. Hypo-allergenic products are

STEPHEN WOLTER

essential for this skin-type and mild cleansing is the key. Light masking should be done no more than twice a week and should be followed by a non-alcoholic toner and lightweight moisturizer (don't forget the neck and bust). Eye cream is also essential. Sensitive skin-types may also suffer irritation from some nail polishes and sun-care products. Sunning and extreme climate changes can play havoc with any skin-type, but sensitive skin must be treated with extra caution. Oil-free and non-waterproof sunblocks (factor 19–30) are advisable. Never go out unprotected.

Combination skin

To some extent, every skin-type is a combination. The usual type, which I am talking about here, has a T-shaped panel of oiliness across the forehead and down the center of the face. Caring for this skin-type can be confusing and expensive—what works on one area may not work on another. Use gentle, non-alcoholic cleansers and toners to maintain skin balance. If pimples should break out, treat only those areas affected, not the whole face. Moisturizer should be lightweight, but a second and slightly richer moisturizer can be used for drier areas. Dual masking may be necessary when treating the T-zone, for example, a clay mask for forehead, nose and chin, and a hydrating mask for cheeks. An eye cream is essential before masking, and should also be used morning and night for extra protection. When out in the sun, use a non-waterproof sunblock (factor 19–30).

Whatever your skin-type, find a facialist who truly cares about your skin and understands the importance of your complexion to your career. Don't be afraid to ask questions—remember, it's your face.

MASKING TIPS

- All skin-types should cleanse thoroughly and apply an eye cream before masking with a suitable product.

- Avoid wearing make-up for 12–24 hours after a facial. This will allow the skin to breathe and benefit from the cleansing treatment.

Skin upsets or dry patches can be a hassle, not only for the model but also for the make-up artist preparing for a tight head shot (close-up). You can help by being aware of the reactions of your skin to such things as flying, changing climates, switching cleansers, changing season, using chlorinated water and sun-bathing. Think before you light another cigarette, have another cocktail or stay up too late. If you think first, you'll never have to ask yourself why your skin looks sluggish, or why you just can't get that red out of your eyes.

GOOD SKIN-CARE HABITS

Regardless of your skin-type, there are several basic steps you can take to maintain clear, healthy skin:

- Always remove make-up before going to bed.
- Apply make-up with clean sponges rather than fingers.
- Don't indulge in "bathroom surgery" (picking at your skin).
- Avoid excessive tanning, outside and on sun-beds.
- Don't steam the skin too frequently.
- Cleanse skin properly.
- Avoid using products not designed for your skin-type.
- Use non-waterproof products which are less likely to clog the pores.
- Don't over-cleanse.
- Use warm water, not hot, for cleansing the face.
- Don't have a professional facial before a tight headshot because the skin will need 2–5 days to heal, depending on skin-type.
- Avoid waxing any facial hair on the day of a headshot as it can cause skin irritation.
- Use a suitable eye cream every night, but do not apply over the lid as it may cause puffiness.
- Get plenty of sleep, especially before headshots, to ensure you look fresh and bright.
- Use non-irritant laundry soaps and fabric softeners.
- Use gentle shampoos which won't irritate the face during rinsing.
- Drink lots of water, preferably bottled and unchlorinated.
- Eat a balanced diet (see Chapter 8).
- Avoid alcohol, tobacco, caffeine, sugar, salt and non-prescribed drugs.

SHAVING FOR MEN

For years men have been advised to shave against the growth of the beard so as to achieve a closer shave. *At no time* should the skin be pulled or stretched—it irritates the skin and increases the risk of ingrown hairs.* Electric shaving greatly reduces the potential for ingrown hairs, and as black skin is more prone to ingrown hairs, I particularly recommend an electric shave for Black male models. If you shave twice a day, alternate between a blade and an electric shaver.

Try to give your skin a rest as often as you can. Always cleanse your face gently after working out, wearing sun care products, powders or light coverages. The color and texture of your skin should remain supple and clean-looking.

*If ingrown hairs are present, gently exfoliate the beard and neck area with a buff puff or cleansing grains before going to bed.

Razor shaving

1 Moisten the skin either by showering first or splashing lukewarm water over the entire beard for several minutes.

2 Apply cream for a dry or tough beard (it softens the hair follicles and helps them remain moist during the entire shave), gel for a sensitive beard and light foam, which is just air, for oily skins or light beards. Massage cream or gel against the growth of the beard, leaving a thin layer on the skin. If using foam, massage in the same way but leave a thick layer on the skin to ensure that the foam won't dry too fast.

3 With a clean, sharp razor, preferably double-edged, begin shaving the cheek area following the growth of the beard. Rinse the razor often with hot water. Finish by shaving the lip and chin area where the hair is generally the thickest, having allowed the cream more time to penetrate and soften the bristles.

If you have any blemishes, follow the above steps, taking care not to cut the irritated skin. You may also find it helpful to apply a bit of mild alcoholic astringent on a cotton ball directly to the razor to disinfect the blade and thus help to reduce the risk of infection. If you nick the skin, press clean, cold cotton against the cut to stop the bleeding. If you bleed profusely when cut, a septic stick may be more effective: dab it on the cut, allow to dry, then gently brush off.

Electric shaving

1 Moisten the beard with lukewarm water.
2 Completely dry the skin.
3 Use a pre-shave product containing alcohol and oil to strengthen the beard and help the blade pick up the bristles easily.

STEPHEN WOLTER

Top *Cleanse the face before shaving.*
Above *Shaving foam can be applied with the fingers or a brush.*
Opposite *Follow the growth of the beard when shaving.*

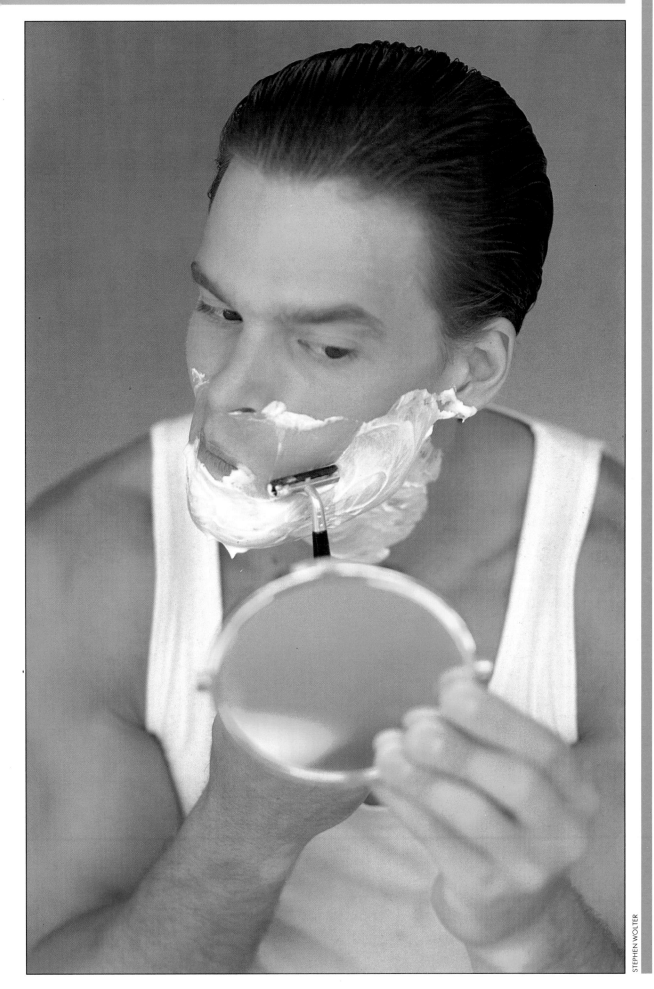

Follow your shave with toner and moisturizer. To avoid irritating the skin, choose products which are low in alcohol and fragrance-free. High collars and woollen fabrics may also be irritating, so be aware of this possible reaction.

FACIAL HAIR (WOMEN)

This subject does not have to be a horror story like the "breakouts" that seem to occur at the most crucial times of your life. There are many effective methods of treating superfluous hair. Usually of most concern are one's eyebrows and "mustache."

Never shave any part of your face. Depilatory products designed for use at home come in the form of creams, foams and gels. Always do a discreet test patch before using any of these products as they sometimes cause irritation.

Bleaching

This method gives only temporary relief as it does not remove the hair but simply lightens its color.

Electrolysis

This is a more permanent way of removing hair. It involves a needle being inserted into the hair root and a small electric shock being applied to kill the follicle. This treatment can be painful and must be continued over a period of time as all the hair cannot be removed in one visit. Possible scarring may occur if not done correctly, so always seek professional help.

Tweezing

Regrowth is rapid with this method and it may cause stubborn ingrown hairs which have the appearance of blackheads. However, it does give you better shaping control for eyebrows. It is unwise to remove a "mustache" by tweezing.

Waxing

Hot waxing opens the pores and grabs the hairs by the root, leaving a smooth finish. Regrowth tends to be slower than with other methods.

Cold waxing takes the hair from the surface and can cause breakage. The finished result is not as smooth as with the hot waxing method and regrowth is faster.

In either case, I suggest professional treatment on a regular basis. I would not recommend you to do this yourself, but if you insist on trying, make sure you seek professional assistance before setting up any kind of waxing method, hot or cold.

SUN CARE

The sun damages your skin: it causes dryness, wrinkles—even cancer. Please don't forget that your face is usually the most exposed area of your body, even when you are not anywhere near a beach. Make the investment of time and money to see which products work best for you and give you maximum protection. The sun protection factor (spf) in any tanning product you purchase should be no less than 19 for the face and chest area and 15 for the body. Avoid waterproof products, which can clog the pores, and oil-based products, which can promote burn.

I do not recommend the use of suntan beds and consider them generally unhealthy for any skin-type. Also avoid homemade tanning products, such as baby oil mixed with iodine, or commercial items, such as tanning blankets or solar reflectors. And let's not forget those hazy summer days—that's when you can really discover what getting burned is all about. A tanned look can be appropriate for modeling swimwear or possibly lingerie, but beware tan lines. They can be difficult to match to the natural skin tone with make-up.

If you still insist on getting a tan, you might want to remember that a tanned look will probably restrict you to a limited marketplace and could even result in loss of work. (A tan tends to make you look "muddy" or "dirty" in black and white photos, so photographers prefer to use pale models and add a tanned effect by using filters.)

If you live in a warm climate and notice any rashes, skin or mole discoloration after being in the sun, consult a dermatologist. Exposure to the sun is known to be a contributory factor in many skin cancers, so take care.

To protect yourself from summer's sun while making rounds, wear natural fibers, such as cotton, linen and silk (they let your skin breathe), wide-brimmed summer hats and UV-approved sunglasses. Don't forget to wear a sunblock with the appropriate protection factor on your face and other exposed areas.

Take care to protect your skin from the sun's harsh rays by wearing a sunscreen and clothing in natural fibers. You don't want to look old before your time.

MAKE-UP
by Darcy McGrath

Your face is a statement to the world, telling people a great deal about the way you think and feel. Your use of cosmetics can indicate your attitude to such things as diet, fashion and self-image. When make-up suits your image and your mood, it makes you look and feel good, thus building confidence and speaking volumes before you've uttered a word. However, confident make-up need not mean heavy application of foundation, eyeliner, mascara and blusher. If you want to enhance your appearance and boost your confidence, read on and learn how to work with cosmetics to your advantage, how to maintain a healthy "glow," and the ultimate goal—how to get your face ready for the camera.

Opposite Clear, glowing skin is always attractive, but even this "look" can be enhanced with make-up applied in natural colors.

The groups of colors on this page are shown with natural objects in the same tones, indicating that you never have to look far for inspiration. All these colors may be used with any skin tone.
Top right The shades of pink here beautifully reflect those found in the pink-veined leaf.
Center left The grays and beiges take their inspiration from the pebbles on a beach.
Bottom left The colors of nature again inspire the delicate shades of peach and pink shown here.
Bottom right Flowers have always been a source of beauty, and these deeper shades of coral and burgundy are reflected in the dried petals of a pot-pourri.

A TYPICAL MAKE-UP SESSION

I like to think of myself as an artist sketching your face. I simply enhance your natural features with one or two colors by working with the colors already in your skin tone. The best effects are achieved by using the color softly.

Regardless of the medium—still photography, television or film—I have found the clean approach in make-up to be the most effective. Unless the lighting is intensely bright and I'm told to create a stronger or brighter make-up, I try to keep the models looking natural. Of course, there are always exceptions due to lighting and the art director's taste. The normal procedure when a girl comes to my chair is as follows.

Assessing skin-type

The first step is to sweep the model's hair away from her face. With clean hands I determine her skin-type and ask her what products she is currently using. Is she using any medicated products? Is she allergic to any cosmetics or beauty aids? Does she have facials, body treatments or any special hair removal techniques?

Preparing skin for make-up

I have her cleanse with the products I know well and trust will work with her skin-type. Afterwards I recheck her skin's texture to ensure smoothness, correcting any problem areas such as dry patches, pimples or stray brow hairs. (Note: I shape

STEPHEN WOLTER

1 Checking skin texture.

2 Exfoliating dry skin layers.

6 Toning the skin with an atomizer of mineral water.

the brows mainly by brushing them. Arching or excessive removal is not complimentary.)

Dry patches are gently removed with a cream-based exfoliator which contains small grains. This *must* be done gently because rubbing too hard overstimulates the skin and causes redness. (This method can also remedy dry lips.)

If there is time (for tight beauty shots I always allow time), I apply a hydrating mask which makes the skin supple. (Oily skin rarely needs this treatment, unless dry patches are visible.) The delicate under-eye area produces little natural oil, so hydrating is particularly beneficial here.

Preparing the eyes
If the eyes appear red, I tilt the model's head back,

close her eyes and apply a saline solution to the inner corner of each eye, being careful not to allow the nozzle of the applicator to come in contact with the eye or skin. When she opens her eyes, the liquid runs inside the eye, not down her face. As an alternative, you can try plain, cool water instead.

Toning and moisturizing
Now I tone the skin with a non-alcoholic toner and 100 percent cotton balls to remove any excess cleanser or previous make-up. Toner restores a proper pH balance to the skin, allowing it to become more receptive to moisturizer. (Misting mineral water over the face is a very good alternative if you don't have a toner; it gets rid of

3 Removing exfoliator with a soft chamois cloth.

4 Brushing the brows to see the natural shape.

5 Inserting eye drops.

7 Applying and delicately blending moisturizer.

8 Rechecking skin texture.

9 Blending foundation around jawline and ear. (This must also be done around the hairline.)

redness and hydrates the surface.) This step creates an occlusive layer between the skin and the moisturizer which prevents the pores clogging quickly, adds suppleness to the skin and helps make-up last longer.

I now apply a lightweight moisturizer over the face and neck. If the eye area needs more moisturizer, I gently pat a light film of eye cream in the under-eye area (not over the lid and not all the way up to the eye itself—that is too irritating to the eye). Do not over-use eye cream at bedtime as it can create puffiness in the morning and cause creasing under make-up.

There are several ways to reduce eye puffiness. Camomile tea bags steeped in hot water, left to cool and then placed over the eyes for 10–15 minutes while the feet are raised is a time-honored remedy, as are cucumber slices. You can also buy herbal-based remedies. If you suffer from prolonged redness or itchiness in the eyes, you may have an infection, so see your optometrist as soon as possible.

If you wear contact lenses, you may choose to leave them in or take them out for beauty shots. (Contacts can be seen in close-ups.) Always carry a storage case as well as your eye solution products. Be sure to tell your make-up artist if you are wearing contacts so she or he can take precautions while working around your eyes.

Choosing and applying foundation

The next step is to determine the foundation for the model's skin tone. (I am a professional and can do this by simply looking at her face. If you are buying foundation, try it on your jawline and examine it in natural light for the best possible choice.)

The key to successfully applying foundation is to keep it as translucent as possible, regardless of skin color. If the foundation is too heavy, mix it with a little moisturizer in your hand to break it down. For a matte finish (and sometimes to save time) I use a powder foundation, which can be applied with a wet sponge or used dry. Liquid foundation should be applied with a damp sponge over the entire face and blended softly into the neck area (unless a high collar is being worn). Always pat—never pull, tug or wipe—when applying. Patting gives more coverage while gliding it over the face makes it sheer.

Covering imperfections

Only work on problem areas after a basic foundation has been applied. Use creamy foundation to help you maintain your natural look. I stay away from extreme highlights which only draw more attention to problem areas.

Under eyes: I dab on a creamy consistency concealer which matches the foundation and let it sit a moment. Do not apply directly into creases as

this will emphasize the lines even more. With an angled sponge, I gently remove excess concealer. **Blemishes, scars, etc:** Use a small eyeliner brush to apply concealer as it enables you to work directly on small areas, achieving a better coverage. Blend away any excess around the edges using the brush. (When it comes to powdering blemished areas later, it must be done very lightly or it can result in immediate dryness to the surface. If this happens, it is very difficult to reapply concealer over the dry spot to make it smooth again.)

Applying blusher

I restore the natural color to the face and redefine its shape with a cream or gel-based blusher. This allows the foundation, color and body temperature to mesh together, creating natural undertones. If, after powdering, I see the need to add more color, I go back over the highlighted areas with a powdered blusher. This gives a smooth finish and avoids the blusher looking as though it's just sitting on top of the skin.

Powdering

The secret of successful powdering is to apply a small amount with a light hand. I use a translucent powder, applying it evenly with a velour puff or sponge over the face and around the eyes and mouth, leaving no residue in corners or creases. To remove any excess, use a puff or sponge, or a large powder brush with sable, pony or goat bristles. Glide the applicator over the foundation so you don't break the texture. Do not apply powder over a powder-based foundation because the skin can become too dry.

Please note that applying a very fair powder to a black skin makes it look ashy, so opt for darker shades in preference.

At this stage in a make-up I do not encourage a lot of facial movement. I want the least amount of creasing for the freshest effect in front of the camera.

> **Note:** It is always best to do smiling shots towards the end of a shoot so head or beauty shots have minimal creasing. Also, the weight of eyewear can cause lines—so save spectacle shots until the end and thus save your face.

Brow definition

To redefine the brows I brush them to see which way they look most natural and then ever so carefully go over *just* the brow (not into the skin) with a moistened brush. If there are gaps in the brow or an uneven shape, they can be corrected by filling in with powder or pencil. I prefer powder for a softer finish. Pencils are fine if you are lighthanded enough. Unruly brows can be tamed

STEPHEN WOLTER

10 Applying concealer under eyes.

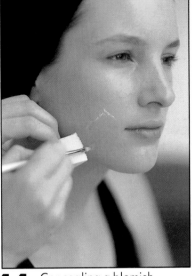

11 Concealing a blemish.

12 Blending concealer with foundation over face.

13 Applying and blending cream blusher.

14 Blending warm tone powder with a sponge.

15 Filling gaps in natural brow shape with powder.

16 Taming unruly brows with a moist mascara wand.

17 Applying natural lip moisturizer.

18 Blending natural tone powder around the eyes with a sponge applicator.

with hair gel or a light application of mascara. Do not remove stray hairs after foundation and powder are applied because this can adversely affect the skin color and texture.

Preparing the lips

First of all I apply a natural gloss, let it sit for a while and then blot it with a non-fibrous tissue or lip paper. This keeps the lips moist and protects the finish, preventing any color bleeding into the skin around the lip area. Final definition is the last step of the make-up session.

Defining the eyes

The first step is to define the eye area with a very natural tone, preferably in a soft brown color—almost camel—as this complements every eye color. I apply it with a brush for a sheer all-over effect. A soft sponge applicator adds more definition in corners and creases. The brush can

come in again to blend the creases and corners smoothly. If definition is necessary under the eye, I apply color either in the lower corners or very sheerly across. The objective is not to draw lines around the eyes but to softly powder around them so the eyes appear first, *not* the make-up. (Hold a puff, sponge or tissue under the lid to avoid excess powder flecking around the under-eye area.)

I now check the model's all over color with the lighting. I make any necessary adjustments regarding the tone, either warming the face with blusher or controlling the natural skin color with foundation and powder. There is nothing worse than over-defined cheeks, mouth and eyes looking totally separate from each other. What you want to accomplish in your coloring is continuity using subtle tones. If additional definition is needed around the eyes, apply it now so you don't leave powder residue on the lashes.

19 Defining around the eyes with a brush.

20 Adding more definition around the eyes.

21 Curling the eyelashes.

23 Separating lashes with a lash comb.

24 Applying lipstick with a lip brush.

25 Blotting lipstick.

Eye make-up

I rarely use eye pencils or mascara on models. Pencils crease too easily and are often applied too heavily. Powders are cleaner-looking. If pencils *are* used, I powder over them with the same color. I like to smudge eyeliner; definite lines are fine for a dramatic effect, but I prefer to keep make-up looking natural and let the model create her own drama.

If your lashes are fair or lack definition without mascara, I recommend having them dyed. (This *must* be done by a professional.) If lashes lack curl, gently use a lash curler *before* mascara is applied to ensure that wet lashes don't become stuck on the curler and get pulled off your eyes.

It is easy to define lashes with mascara. Start at the top of the upper lash and do the underside; this gives the effect of length and an invisible liner look. Redefine the bottom lashes with a very thin coat. I always try to use the sheerest amount of non-fibrous, non-waterproof mascara because it remains clean and unclumpy. If lashes should stick together, a lash comb or separator easily separates them. Do this while they are still wet. I generally use black or dark brown mascara. Color mascaras are great for various effects, but do not contribute to a natural finish.

Lip definition

The final step is to look at the lip color and determine what tones are already present. I want to bring out that color as clearly and naturally as possible. I again go over the lips with the chosen color and then blot the excess; this reduces shine and keeps it from bleeding outside the natural lip line. (Note: If you go outside the natural lip line with a shiny finish, you draw more attention to the correction. If you use a matte lip color, a lip pencil used over the entire lip area or a blotted lip color, the correction is less obvious.)

22 Applying mascara to top lashes.

26 Right The finished make-up.

STEPHEN WOLTER

Make-up variations for Black models

Darker skin may need greater definition around the eye area. Deeper shades can be applied above the lid as well as below; applying a lighter shade under the darker liner helps to soften the liner effect.

Foundation and powder choice are crucial to darker skin tones. Too light a foundation and powder can cause a chalky effect, so always choose the most natural tones to complement your look.

Use a natural color on the lips, but do not paint an exaggerated outline. On the cheeks, use a sheer, translucent color as this always has the most natural effect, no matter what the skin tone.

1 *Applying black eyeliner with a brush.*
2 *Softly applying black liner to the corners of the eyes.*
3 *"Softening" the liner by applying brown tone under the eyes.*
4 *The finished make-up.*

STEPHEN WOLTER

The color schemes shown below can be used in any combination, as long as you use the correct shades for your skin tone. The most commonly used colors are warm browns, pinks and peaches, but color schemes can be varied to suit your mood or match your clothes.
Left *Peaches and pinks, shown here on light skin.*
Right *Browns and beiges, shown here on Oriental skin.*
Bottom *Deep pinks and browns, shown here on Black skin.*

67

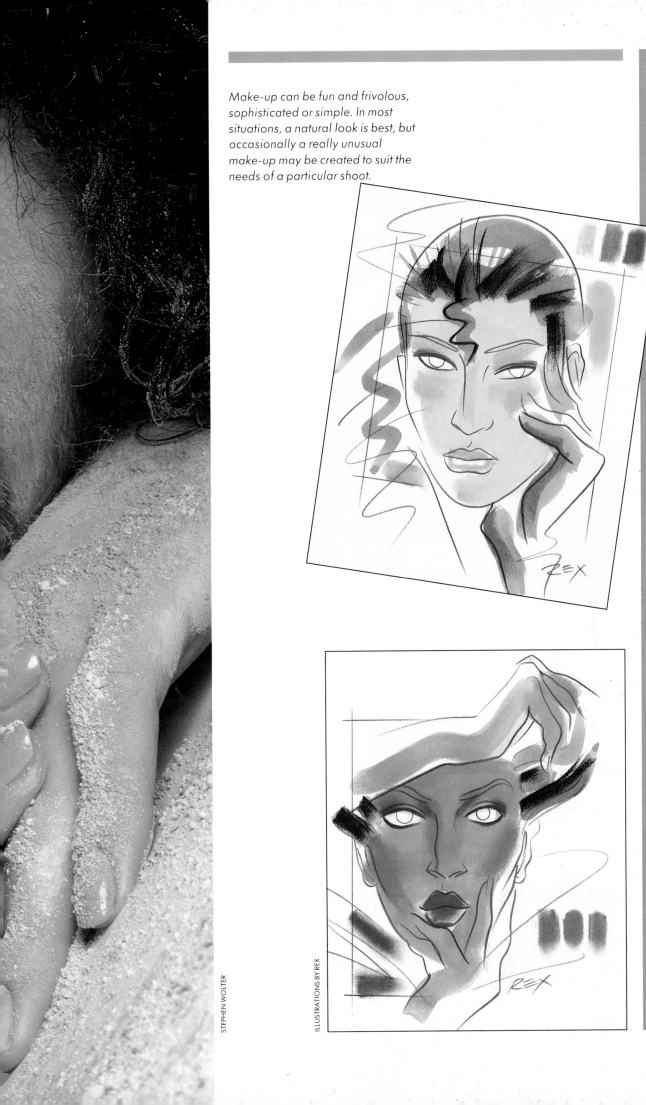

Make-up can be fun and frivolous, sophisticated or simple. In most situations, a natural look is best, but occasionally a really unusual make-up may be created to suit the needs of a particular shoot.

STEPHEN WOLTER

ILLUSTRATIONS BY REX

69

BEAUTY EQUIPMENT

Good quality skin-care products, make-up, brushes, nail kit, carrying bag and other miscellaneous items, are both a personal and a business investment. Although the initial outlay is costly, these items are tax-deductible, so keep all your receipts. It is your professional responsibility to maintain your looks, so invest in the proper care and enjoy yourself while doing it.

Brushes

When selecting brushes for your kit, you must come to one decision right off – quality not quantity. I am very choosy about my brushes: I look for firmness and a medium width in a lip brush, and soft rounded shapes in eye brushes so I can blend creases and corners. I also like soft and foamy, rounded sponge eye applicators. A thin, firm eyeliner brush can be used for concealing blemishes, as well as lining the eyes. A soft toothbrush is great for eyebrows. Find non-prickly blusher brushes that feel like silk on your face at any angle. Powder brushes should

be full with the same silky feeling. Handle-length varies, so choose a length you feel comfortable using. The hair can range from sable (the most expensive) to pony and goat.

All brushes should be washed regularly with mild soaps designed for the skin. Shape and stack them in an upright position or lay them flat on a towel to dry.

Several companies manufacture brush sets, but very few are of dependable quality, so I prefer to buy them individually. Do shop around before you make your purchases as prices vary considerably.

Other tools

Velour puffs are great and can be washed the same way as brushes. The sewn puffs last longer and once washed are very pliable.

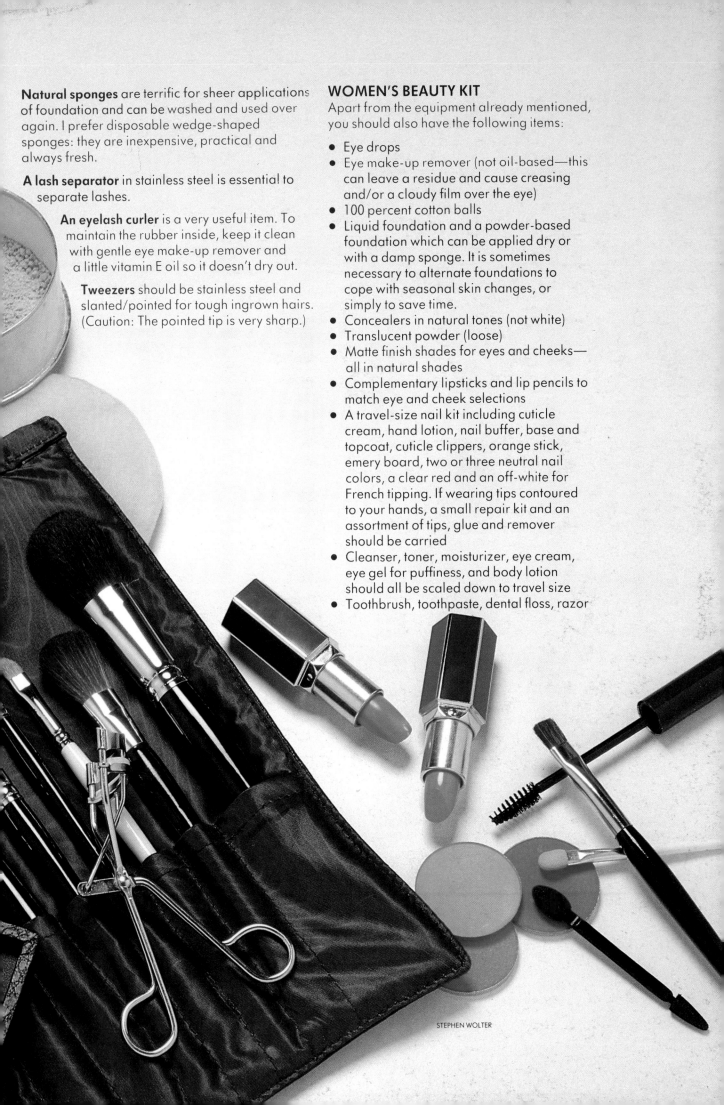

Natural sponges are terrific for sheer applications of foundation and can be washed and used over again. I prefer disposable wedge-shaped sponges: they are inexpensive, practical and always fresh.

A lash separator in stainless steel is essential to separate lashes.

An eyelash curler is a very useful item. To maintain the rubber inside, keep it clean with gentle eye make-up remover and a little vitamin E oil so it doesn't dry out.

Tweezers should be stainless steel and slanted/pointed for tough ingrown hairs. (Caution: The pointed tip is very sharp.)

WOMEN'S BEAUTY KIT

Apart from the equipment already mentioned, you should also have the following items:

- Eye drops
- Eye make-up remover (not oil-based—this can leave a residue and cause creasing and/or a cloudy film over the eye)
- 100 percent cotton balls
- Liquid foundation and a powder-based foundation which can be applied dry or with a damp sponge. It is sometimes necessary to alternate foundations to cope with seasonal skin changes, or simply to save time.
- Concealers in natural tones (not white)
- Translucent powder (loose)
- Matte finish shades for eyes and cheeks— all in natural shades
- Complementary lipsticks and lip pencils to match eye and cheek selections
- A travel-size nail kit including cuticle cream, hand lotion, nail buffer, base and topcoat, cuticle clippers, orange stick, emery board, two or three neutral nail colors, a clear red and an off-white for French tipping. If wearing tips contoured to your hands, a small repair kit and an assortment of tips, glue and remover should be carried
- Cleanser, toner, moisturizer, eye cream, eye gel for puffiness, and body lotion should all be scaled down to travel size
- Toothbrush, toothpaste, dental floss, razor

STEPHEN WOLTER

MEN'S GROOMING KIT

- Cleanser
- Toner
- Facial moisturizer
- Eye balm or cream
- Non-waxy lip balm with sunscreen
- 100 percent cotton balls
- Razors (standard twin-blade disposables and a rechargeable electric razor able to remove sideburns)
- Shaving gel, cream or foam
- Shaving brush
- Natural tone concealer
- Powder
- Body lotion
- Nail kit (buffing cream, buffer, orange stick, nail file, white stick to whiten tips lightly, nail clippers)
- Tweezers
- Small scissors
- Toothbrush to shape brows
- Toothbrush, toothpaste and dental floss

STEPHEN WOLTER

HAIR
by Judith Gold

Hair is one of the most important aspects of your appearance. It can be your crowning glory or a clear giveaway that you don't spend enough time on your grooming.

For bookings or auditions you will be expected to arrive with hair that is clean, shiny and in excellent condition. Beyond the obvious photogenic advantages, hair that is well cared for is also better able to cope with regular assaults from gels, lotions, mousses and sprays, hairdryers, heated rollers, curling tongs and crimping irons. Your hair will be brushed, teased, spiked, pinned, braided, twisted or even made to stand on end, if that is what the situation calls for. Torture is not the intention. A hairdresser's job is to make you look your best, molding you into the image desired by the photographer or client. You can help by having a cooperative attitude and a very open mind.

To learn all that is necessary, find a hairdresser you can trust and talk to—one who understands the modeling business. Ask other models and your agency for referrals. They will give you recommendations from personal experience. Once you have determined the best choice, make an appointment lengthy enough to discuss your needs before any services are performed.

For your first appointment, take photographs of haircuts and styles you like. These will show exactly what you have in mind and prevent misunderstandings.

Opposite *Beautiful hair like this is a terrific asset, but it rarely comes about on its own. It's essential to find a good hairdresser who will advise you how to care for your hair and recommend suitable products.*
Below *Bizarre hairstyles can be part of a normal day's work. Provided you look after your hair, it will happily survive whatever "punishment" is heaped on it.*

STEPHEN WOLTER

WOMEN'S HAIRSTYLES

There are five basic types of haircut, each with numerous styling possibilities.

Long, one-length hair

This is usually cut to the collar, shoulder or mid-back length. It can be styled loose and natural, casually braided, pulled back into a pony-tail or hairclips, or swept up into a sleek, sophisticated look.

One length with a bang

A bang brings softness to the face and allows more styling flexibility. You can achieve height and fullness easily because the hair is shorter at the front hairline, yet still long enough elsewhere to pull back or put up.

Long layered hair

This cut is usually shoulder length at the back with shorter layers around the face and on top. As layers remove weight from the top, this haircut allows long hair to be softer or fuller.

Geometric cuts

These cuts can be very short to medium-length wedges, or "bob" styles. They have very distinctive shapes and look quite individual.

Short, layered hair

This is very short all over with the top layers no longer than 3–4in (these layers will add height or fullness on top). Layered cuts can be styled to look spiky or sleek, brushed back off the face or all brushed forward for a soft wispy effect. They can be very casual or very sophisticated.

CHOOSING A HAIRSTYLE

As you can see, each length of hair has many styling alternatives. How do you select the right one for you? These are the factors hairdressers take into consideration when helping to make your choice:

Your agency's recommendations

They have a knowledge of clients' preferences and how your look will best fit your career.

STEPHEN WOLTER

The five basic cuts: geometric; long, one-length; one-length with a bang; short layers; long layers.

Variations on a basic layered cut:
1 Short, layered hair looking casual and natural.
2 A neat variation on the basic cut.
3 A sleeker look – slicked back with gel.
4 This sophisticated spiked look is created with styling mousse.

STEPHEN WOLTER

Facial analysis

Your hairdresser can take you step-by-step and show you how and why each type of cut would be right or wrong for your face. He or she can also show you how to adapt almost any cut to work with your facial features.

Body proportions

A haircut can look great for your face, but wrong for your body size. For example, crew cut hair on a model six feet tall could appear ridiculously out of proportion. Very long hair on a petite model can sometimes be overpowering. Your body size and height are important factors in choosing a hairstyle.

Hair texture and type

Is your hair straight, wavy or curly? Fine, limp, thick or coarse? Fine hair needs a more defined shape and layers help achieve fullness that one-length cuts will not. Straight hair works better than curly hair for one-length cuts because it will lie smoothly; curly hair will tend to look frizzy. Wavy/curly hair works best in soft layered looks

77

(long or short). Layering will control the fullness and allow more styling possibilities (curly hair can be blow-dried smooth for a change and the curl will give it body).

Many ethnic groups have different hair textures. These differences are important to know because they sometimes have special needs.

Oriental and Hispanic hair is usually very coarse and straight. It looks beautiful when it is kept natural and in prime condition.

Black hair ranges from very fine to coarse, and from wavy to frizzy. At one time, most Black models straightened their hair. Now, the possibilities are endless. The hair can be gently relaxed, completely straightened, or permed on large rods to turn frizzy textures into soft curls. These chemical changes should always be done professionally.

If your hair is too fragile to grow long, you might like to invest in hair-weaving or extensions. This technique is expensive and must be done only by an expert. It involves weaving hair into your own and must be redone periodically as it grows away from your scalp with your natural hair growth. However, it is easy to care for as you simply shampoo and condition as usual.

For all types of ethnic hair, it is essential to use good hair-care and styling products. Those which work best on Caucasian hair may have no effect. Be sure the hairdresser you choose is very knowledgeable about your particular needs and ask for product recommendations in the following categories:

- Shampoo/conditioner
- Wet styling
- Blow-drying for curl
- Blow-drying to straighten
- Curl activators
- Finish and shine

Note: Once you have found the products that work best for you, keep them in your model's bag and don't hesitate to show them to the photo hairdresser. I can tell you from experience, it helps when models give me detailed information about their hair. That way we can work together to create a fabulous look!

Hair texture varies among different ethnic types and can be altered with various chemical processes. From left to right Naturally straight Oriental hair; gently relaxed Black hair; naturally curled Black hair; permed Caucasian hair; straightened Black hair.

78

CHANGING HAIR TEXTURE

It is possible to change the texture of your hair by using permanent waves and chemical relaxers (straighteners). These chemicals actually alter the structure of your hair (new hair growth is unaffected). They can be very harsh, and combined with the everyday workout a model's hair can have, this does not lead to a very healthy or luxurious head of hair. If you insist on having them, perms and relaxers *must be done professionally* and *only when absolutely necessary*. You might consider these treatments if your hair is so limp that a very soft body wave will add a little fullness (not curl). Alternatively, if your hair does not curl, but frizzes, a mild relaxer will give it some control. Uneven curl patterns can be balanced with a jumbo rod body wave.

MEN'S HAIRSTYLES

The male model needs the same professional advice as his female counterpart. After getting a referral from his agency, he should book a lengthy first appointment with a professional hairdresser. During the consultation he will need to ask lots of questions.

Men's haircuts are the most important aspect of

ILLUSTRATIONS BY REX

Left to right *Short, layered hair with close-cropped sides; longer layers just skimming the ears; one length to ears and cut close into neck; long layered hair; long one-length hair.*

80

their grooming because they single-handedly dictate a man's style or "look." In view of this, it is essential for male model agencies to understand the relevant markets and what "looks" will sell.

There have been many changes in men's hair fashions. But a style acceptable in one business could be a disaster for a model and perhaps lose him big bookings. Always get your agency's advice before getting a close-shaved "buzz" cut, or deciding to keep you hair shoulder length. Once these extreme fashion trends are "out," you might have to make a change.

Generally speaking, perms and straightening treatments are "no-nos" for men. However, some hair textures require help to make them manageable. Ask your hairdresser for guidance.

Short hair

Most male models wear variations of a short, layered cut:
1 1–3in long on top with very close-cropped sides and neckline. This cut is great because it can look very conservative, or be spiked into a more fun style.
2 3–5in long on top with hair over the top of the ears and 1–2in long at the neckline. This style is slightly more casual because of the extra length—but gel can transform this cut into a very sleek European look.
3 4–6in long on top with close-cropped sides and neckline. This shape takes on a more avant garde, geometric look when blow-dried. When styled with gels or lotions, it can look very sophisticated.

Longer hair

There are two main ways of treating longer hair on men:
1 Long-layered—usually collar or shoulder length. These cuts are usually better on naturally curly or wavy hair. (Straight layered hair would not be as full.) This cut has a very casual look.
2 One-length—hair must be in excellent condition to sell this look. It can be styled loose or slicked into a braid or ponytail. Again, check with your agency. Many models are finding that they cannot work in the US with hair this long.

Styling possibilities and techniques for men

Achieving different looks for each haircut is not difficult, and the possibilities are endless. This is where your hairdresser becomes very important. Your haircut must be followed by a lesson in styling techniques:

- Blow-drying
- Use of gel, mousse, lotion and spray
- Wet styling

By learning these techniques and practicing on yourself, you will be prepared for any booking. Remember to pay attention and ask questions while having your hair done. Hairdressers can give you lots of valuable information.

Men's hair care

Having hair that is clean and in top condition is critical for a successful career. The camera only too easily reveals hair which has been neglected. For optimum results, get professional advice on shampoos, conditioners and styling products best suited to your individual needs. Most of all, be consistent in your hair care.

MAINTENANCE AND EASE OF STYLING

For both men and women, you've now seen how each length of hair can be styled many different ways, but how easy or difficult will it be to achieve these looks? How often will your hair have to be cut to maintain its shape? These factors are very important because *you* will need to be able to do a lot of your own styling on a day-to-day basis. A good stylist will make sure your look is easy to care for and give you a lesson incorporating all styling possibilities.

HAIR COLOR

If you have beautiful hair color naturally, leave it that way. A dark lustrous brunette is just as valuable as a blonde or redhead. (Men rarely need to change hair color, unless their natural color is too drab.) Avoid color that is too trendy or outrageous and changing your color too often. If you do the latter, your clients will never know if you're going to be right for a particular booking. If you were a blonde when they last saw you and you show up this time as a redhead, they might not be able to use you. Subtle change is the key—a little lighter, slightly darker, or discreet highlights can work beautifully to enhance the look your clients like. That is exactly what hair color is all about—bringing out the best of the natural you. Choosing the type of color depends on the effect you wish to achieve.

Permanent hair color

Highlights are achieved by applying a coloring agent to small sections of hair pulled through a rubber cap, or wrapped in foil. This will achieve a brighter, almost sun-lightened effect, which can be subtle or dramatic. A tint one or two shades *lighter* than your own color gives it a beautiful soft shine, picking up the natural highlights of your hair. It will brighten drab blondes and reds, and will give a beautiful auburn highlight to dark brown shades. Bleach is used when you want a more dramatic change.

Approximately 90 percent of color used on models is achieved by using a highlighting technique. Not only does it brighten the color, but it gives shine under studio lights and adds body to the hair. When applied properly, highlighting does not give a strong outgrowth around the hairline, and only needs to be maintained about every 2–4 months, depending on the growth of the hair.

Lowlights are achieved by the same technique as highlights. The difference is that a tint, one or two *shades* darker than your own, is used to add more depth. This is an excellent way to make your color

slightly darker, or to allow previously lightened hair to grow out more gracefully.

Tints put color all over your hair for a complete color change and require touch-ups every 3–5 weeks. This is not usually recommended for models unless you have a high percentage of gray hair that needs to be covered.

Semi-permanent color

This is usually applied like a shampoo, covered with a plastic bag and left on for 20–40 minutes. It leaves no outgrowth line and gradually fades from the hair. The more often you shampoo, the faster it fades. This color is a great way to blend, rather than cover, gray hair, or to give all-over highlights to your own color. It does not change the natural color; it simply leaves a coating on the hair.

STEPHEN WOLTER

Above A coloring agent is applied to the hair, which is then wrapped in foil. Right The result is subtle highlights which add shine and natural-looking color.

Color glaze is a tint mixed with a little peroxide. This only enhances your natural highlights; it does not change your hair color. It lasts 3–4 weeks and is an ideal way to see if you like having color.

Condition color is a tint mixed with a moisturizing conditioner to add more shine and luster to your natural color. It will fade out gradually in 2–4 weeks, but the conditioning benefits will linger on if proper hair care is followed. (This is a great way to restore sun-bleached hair.)

Henna is made from a natural plant substance and acts like a staining agent on the hair. It does not change your natural color, but simply coats the hair. It is applied as a thick, green paste and covered with a plastic bag for 30–60 minutes, depending how easily your hair takes the color. Using a hairdryer can speed up the process.

Henna will gradually fade out of the hair. It should not be applied more often than every three months because it can have a build-up effect which will leave you with dry hair and brassy color. Applied at three-month intervals, it will leave your hair shiny with a wonderful translucent color glow.

Temporary color

This is used for quick color changes as it shampoos completely out of your hair leaving no effect. Temporary colors can be used for fun changes for photos or parties and are a good way to try color before you do it permanently.

Rinses are applied after shampooing. They are combed through the hair before styling and add color highlights to medium and dark shades. They can also be used to tone highlighted or naturally light shades of hair.

STEPHEN WOLTER

83

Colored mousse adds subtle or vivid color highlights, also giving light control to the hair.

Colored gel adds subtle or vivid highlights and gives extra control to the hair.

Colored hairsprays can be applied gently or heavily to completely coat the hair with color. They come in every conceivable shade and have the hold of a firm spray.

Note: Colored mousse, gel and hairspray should not be used on bleached or very light hair colors. They have a staining effect and are difficult to remove.

Permanent and semi-permanent color should be applied by a professional hairdresser. The money you might save by doing it yourself cannot make up for the disasters you might create. It could cost you double your saving to have the color

Colored mousse is a simple method of applying temporary color to the hair. It washes out easily so it's great for experimenting.

STEPHEN WOLTER

corrected (not to mention the bookings you could lose in the meantime). Before you leave the salon, ask about special shampoos and conditioners for color-treated hair. They will protect your hair from dryness and prevent your beautiful new color from fading too quickly.

HAIR CARE AND MAINTENANCE

Remember the last time you saw a great-looking head of hair in a shampoo and conditioner commercial on television? That kind of hair does not just happen—it is achieved by following a daily or weekly regime prescribed for your individual needs. Keep it simple, using no more than three or four products in all.

Shampoo

Yes, it does matter what shampoo you use. Curly and coarse hair need a more moisturizing shampoo than fine hair. Fine hair needs a gentler one than oily hair. Some are better for color-treated or permed hair. Ask your hairdresser for guidance. And, no, you don't need to switch shampoos because your hair "gets used to it"— only when the seasons change and you may need more or less moisture.

Hair should be washed as often as necessary to keep it clean. For some that means every day, for others perhaps once or twice a week.

Conditioners

Deep conditioner is used to strengthen damaged hair and maintain healthy hair. It must be left in the hair for 10–20 minutes before rinsing thoroughly.

Moisturizing conditioner replaces moisture lost by heat damage (hairdryers, curling irons, heated rollers). This treatment should be used 3–4 times a week for very dry hair and 2–3 times a week for slightly dry hair. For those with an oily scalp, but dry hair, only condition the ends of the hair.

Superpac or Reconstructive conditioner contains moisturizers and protein to help strengthen hair damaged by too many perms, relaxers or color changes. This conditioner is also very good for weak, fragile hair as the protein makes it stronger. This treatment may be used 3–4 times a week for extremely damaged hair and 2–3 times a month for fragile or slightly damaged hair.

Conditioning rinse is a quick conditioner applied to the hair for 1–3 minutes before rinsing. It should be used after every shampoo (except when a deep-conditioning treatment is applied). This type of product removes tangles and static electricity and leaves the hair very shiny. Please note that a conditioning rinse does not take the place of a regular deep-conditioning treatment.

STEPHEN WOLTER

Conditioning is a must for all hair types. Choose a product recommended by your hairdresser and use it regularly to keep your hair in tip-top condition.

Surface build-up remover is used to remove the accumulated effects of gels, hairsprays, certain conditioners and chlorine from the surface of your hair. It is applied to wet hair for one minute, then rinsed out. Shampoo and conditioner are then applied. For swimmers this should be done after each time in the pool. For other build-up problems, use once or twice a month.

Caring for your hair is not a difficult task. With the proper advice, and just a little of your time, you can have fabulous hair.

STYLING

Now that your hair is in great shape, you'll need some tips on how to achieve the styles you like. Naturally, the more you practice, the easier it will become.

Blow-drying

When hair is very wet, bend over and dry it upside down. Stand up and dry the ends in the appropriate direction when the hair is almost dry. This will add more volume to your hair.

If using gel, mousse or lotion, apply it *before* drying to give hair more body and control.

Note that using a brush when drying will give a smoother effect; using a finger-drying or "scrunching" technique will give a more textured effect. A diffuser on your hairdryer will dry curly or wavy hair without straightening or frizzing it.

Heated rollers are one of the quickest methods to put curl in your hair. To use, take large sections of hair and make partings at an angle (from ear to crown) so that your style will not separate. Leave the rollers in for 5–15 minutes, depending on how much curl you want, then brush thoroughly. Always unwind rollers—pulling them will tear and break your hair.

Curling irons are quick, but rather difficult to use on yourself. Be sure all the ends of the hair are inside the iron before curling, or they will be bent instead of smooth. **Crimping** and **waving irons** are available for more unusual effects. **Straightening irons** will give sleeker hair.

Styling aids

Mousse is a light foam that gives control and slight body to the hair. It can be used when blow-drying, or applied to the hair before letting it dry naturally.

Gel is used when greater hold and control are needed. It works equally well when blow-drying or slicking back the hair into a more sculpted, sophisticated look. Gel is also good for accentuating spiked or curly textures in the hair.

Styling lotion ranges from a soft conditioning spray that protects the hair from heat (blow-drying and setting) and leaves it naturally silky, to a strong designing spray that allows you to style the hair straight up on end if necessary. This is highly recommended for fine hair because it is not as heavy as gel and won't weigh hair down.

Hairspray holds your hair in place after styling. It is available in many different strengths, so select one that suits the amount of hold your style needs.

Blow-drying hair upside-down will give it more body.

STEPHEN WOLTER

STEPHEN WOLTER

1 Heated rollers are a quick way of adding curl to your hair.

2 Hair benders are soft, pliable rods used on damp hair to give loose curls.

3 A waving iron is very useful for creating unusual effects.

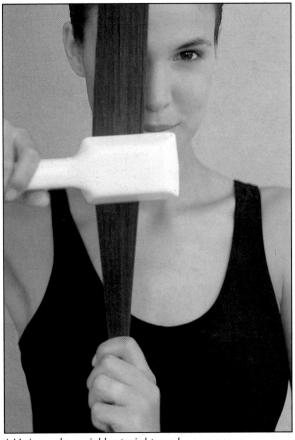

4 Hair can be quickly straightened with a flattening iron.

MANICURE AND PEDICURE

I am indebted to Debbie Ciampi of Viva Nails in Chicago for giving me the benefit of her experience in writing this section. As this is not a beauty book, I am not giving you a photo-by-photo explanation of a manicure and pedicure, but I will give you a few tips. By this time in your life you should have a basic knowledge on how to care for your nails. If not, find yourself a good manicurist and learn. This is another investment to bring you closer to perfection in your modeling career.

I have had manicures around the world and have come to the conclusion that the best are electric manicures. The most significant difference is that, unlike ordinary manicures, the nails are not soaked. As far as the finished manicure is concerned, I find that nail polish stays on longer and rarely chips. In an electric manicure, old polish is removed in the conventional way with a cotton ball soaked in remover. An emery board is used to file the nails into a slightly square shape (to strengthen the sides), cuticle cream is applied around the cuticles, then a small, hand-held electric machine with a specially shaped tip gently pushes back the cuticles. The cream is removed with a paper towel, then cuticle oil is applied, again using the pusher as the massager. Next, nail cream is applied and a rotating electric brush scrubs the surface of the nails to clean them and remove unwanted residue. You then wash your hands, using a soapy nail brush to scrub off the creams and oil, and dry with a paper towel. Hang nails (only) are clipped, then it's time for the polish: one clear base coat and two color coats. After ten minutes' drying time, a clear sealer is applied. This manicure generally lasts me 7–10 days, even though my hands get rough treatment from constantly working with papers at my desk.

A pedicure is basically the same process, but time is allowed for removing hard skin and massaging the feet.

NAIL CARE TIPS

- Keep polish on nails, even if it is clear—it keeps them strong and looking nicer.
- Change polish weekly.
- Keep hands well creamed, especially during winter months.
- Put cuticle oil on dry cuticles at least once a day—twice during winter.

- Don't remove any artificial (sculptured) nails by yourself—get a manicurist.
- Never use any metal instruments on your nails—they scrape away proteins.

If you can afford it, invest in an electric manicure set. It does the job faster and the finished result lasts longer than conventional manicures. If you cannot afford a machine, try to find a manicurist who uses the electric manicure method.

DENTAL CARE

This is by far the most common cosmetic work in the modeling business. Under harsh lighting and in close-up work gaps, chips, stains, discolored fillings, poorly fitting crowns and badly placed teeth become more obvious. Some problems, like chipped or pointed ("fang") teeth can be smoothed down or rounded off very inexpensively. Modern dental materials now enable you to have white fillings, and the same substance can be used to fill gaps between your teeth. Porcelain laminate or plastic facings (bonding) can be used to cover ugly front teeth without doing any damage to them, but they can

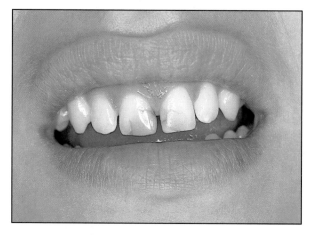

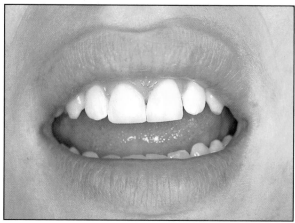

ROD McNEIL

Discolored teeth are a common problem, but can be easily and inexpensively corrected. In this case, tooth-colored plastic has been used to cover unsightly areas and fill gaps to give an even appearance and color.

never be considered as permanent and may need replacing over the years.

Whatever you do, don't be persuaded to have expensive and destructive crown and bridge work unless there is nothing else that can be done. Remember, teeth can make or break a model's career, so do not have any photos taken until your teeth do you justice. Ask your agent's advice and consult at least two dentists to get independent opinions and quotations—they may well differ in their advice.

PERSONAL HYGIENE

It might seem silly to write about personal hygiene, but if it were unnecessary I wouldn't mention it.

Many countries think that women with hairy legs and armpits are beautiful; this does not hold true in fashion photography. A model should always shave legs and armpits before any photo session. As a safeguard, keep soap and a razor in your bag. Men should always be freshly shaved, unless the client has made a specific request for stubble—some clients like the one-day growth look. Men should also be prepared to shave if necessary and travel equipped to do so.

When it comes to menstruation, women should use tampons or the slim pads that attach to the inside of panties. The old-fashioned pad and belt can show through clothing and spoil otherwise beautiful photographs.

Deodorants are always necessary for both men and women, although some clients in certain countries do not like perfumed armpits because of the risk of staining. Be sure to use a deodorant that will not spoil the client's garments. Women can wear dress shields for added protection.

Underwear may seem an obvious thing to wear, but you'd be surprised how many people don't. If you don't wear it, you must always carry a selection of underwear in your bag. It is not the stylist's responsibility to provide your personal undergarments.

Brushing the teeth! Yes, boys and girls, there are some people who do not enjoy this ritual. They choose to walk around with bad breath and bits of food stuck in their teeth—very distasteful and embarrassing. After eating, always check your mouth. And if you're going to do a tight shot with another model, please use a breath freshener: it can be very difficult for another model to concentrate with bad breath filling the air.

PLASTIC SURGERY

Do not have plastic surgery performed just because of your career. If you feel insecure about yourself physically and surgery will help, only then should you consider it. What if you have surgery

> *Be very careful in selecting your surgeon. You have to be able to talk to him. Get more than one opinion. Speak with the patients of your chosen surgeon. Ask to see before and after pictures of his surgery. Also check with the American Academy of Cosmetic Surgery, or any other cosmetic surgical association if you're in need of some referrals in your area.*
>
> Dr Richard Caleel
> President-elect, 1989–90
> American Academy of Cosmetic Surgery

just to please someone else and it goes wrong? What will happen to your career and yourself?

I have interviewed many models who have been advised by agents to have nose jobs, breast implants, chin implants, cheek implants . . . My goodness, there's a lot of free advice out there on how aspiring models can change themselves. I think that we should work with the original product and exhaust all possibilities before you go under the knife.

If you have seriously considered the consequences and you choose to have cosmetic surgery, you must do extensive research and ask your agent to find you a reputable surgeon. The most common types of surgery are breast implants and nose alterations.

Models make more money if they do lingerie, so the incentive for having breast surgery is often financial. The rate of pay may be time and a half, double or even triple, depending upon the item being shot. (Lingerie normally requires a 34B bra, sometimes 34C. The requirement is smaller for young teen models.)

Nose alterations are probably the most commonplace surgery. I know one model who had her nose done three times. The second time was because the first surgeon had not done a good job. The third time was due to the scar tissue not healing properly; the nose photographed strangely. We tried to talk her out of it the third time. We thought that it would eventually fall off her face. She didn't listen, she went ahead. The third surgery was perfect—her nose looks great and you can barely tell there was any surgery. However, I know of some models who didn't have her success . . .

I do not encourage any type of surgery until you have really thought it out and are certain you wish to change something for yourself and not for your career. The dangers are too real to ignore, so please be very careful before you do anything to alter yourself.

DAN ZAITZ

CHAPTER 4

ETIQUETTE

In the agency
•
In the studio
•
Go-sees and auditions
•
On the telephone
•
Socializing
•
Courtesies

How you conduct yourself in both
business and social contexts is very
important if you want to make the right
impression and have people regard you
professionally.

The following information on etiquette may seem obvious but, unfortunately, is often neglected. Please read it very carefully. You are establishing your reputation, so begin your new career with good habits.

Common sense and consideration towards others are necessary elements for success, regardless of your career. As you enter and leave agencies, studios and client interviews, use the telephone or socialize it is imperative that you keep the following points in mind.

IN THE AGENCY

The modeling agency is the nerve center of the business—a pressure cooker of constant activity. Phones ring continuously with inquiries from aspiring and established models, new clients, current clients, make-up artists, hairdressers, photographers, art directors, messengers, talent scouts, out-of-town modeling agencies, parents and friends. People flow in and out of the office. Bookers and agents within the agency also need to talk to each other. Everyone needs attention. Then, you call or walk into the agency wanting attention . . .

Do not take it personally if your booker does not have time to spend with you immediately. Yes, you are important, but if you do not have urgent business, you'll have to take a number. However, we are not mind-readers. If you do have an emergency then you must speak up, even if only to the receptionist; she'll know what to do or who you should speak to if your booker is swamped with priorities.

Bookers wear many hats, often acting as psychiatrists, surrogate parents, best friends, financial advisers, rental agents, best and worst critics and chauffeurs, to name just a few. Imagine trying to be everything to everyone at once. It can be very draining. A simple "please" and "thank you" will work wonders with them. Be considerate and patient. The more considerate you are of them the more they will be of you. Do not assume they will always solve all your problems. They also have their own to deal with.

Go in and out of the agency as quickly as possible. It is very disturbing to have a lot of people just hanging around. You should not have extra time on your hands. What else could you be doing? Preparing for a photo session? Taking a client out to lunch? Looking for a part-time job? Taking dance lessons? Working out at the gym? Taking acting lessons? Keep busy! (Can you imagine how many IBM computers would be sold if the salesmen just hung around the office—not a lot!) A model is a salesperson—you must always be out selling yourself. You cannot rely on your agency for everything.

Do not make any calls on the agency phone unless you are given permission. Agencies provide many services, most of which are free. However, there are some for which reimbursement is expected: overnight messengers, inner-city messengers, overseas phone calls, telexes, portfolios and composites, rent for the agency apartment, or any other special service that may incur a high cost to the agency.

The agency is not a bank! Do not expect advances or interest-free loans. I've been in this business for nine years now. It is amazing to me and my colleagues that models assume we exist to finance them. This is not true. You are responsible for your own career whatever line of business you are in.

IN THE STUDIO

You must treat a photographer's studio as if it were his or her home—very often it is. Remember that you are welcomed inside with the understanding that you will respect the property and the environment.

- Always be professional. Never forget that you are there to work, no matter how friendly the atmosphere.

- You may offer to bring coffee or croissants to the shoot. You may be told it is not necessary, but the thought will be remembered and appreciated.

- Be prepared. You should always arrive with your requested wardrobe intact, pressed and clean. Always bring your model's bag. Don't rely on any other person, such as the stylist, make-up artist or hairdresser to cover for you.

- Personal stereos do not allow you to hear if someone is calling you. If you want something to pass the time while waiting to go on set, take a book to read.

- Arrive promptly at the time specified. You may develop a close relationship with various studios and they might allow you to arrive early. Always telephone first to ask—don't assume.

- Introduce yourself to everyone when you arrive. Be friendly. Shyness often comes across as arrogance. Write down the names and occupations of everyone in the studio: photographer, studio manager, photo assistant, make-up artist, hairdresser, art director/client and other models.

- Always ask before you take or use anything that does not belong to you.

- Don't send the photo assistant to run errands for you. If there is an emergency, always ask the photographer before getting an employee to leave the studio.

- When changing, take care not to get make-up on the clothes you are to model. Get them on and off as quickly as possible and *hang them up* immediately.

- Ask the stylist about wearing dress shields to prevent perspiration stains.

- Don't sit, eat or smoke while wearing the client's clothes. They are often the only samples and have taken a long time to press.

- If you like the garment you are modeling, you may ask the studio manager about purchasing it—after the photo session. Do not assume you can take it and do not pressure the client to give it to you. This will really put you in bad standing.

- Watch your step while walking on and off the set. There are many cords, lights and other equipment that you could stumble on. Be careful!

- Don't chat with the other models on set. This is very distracting for the photographer and will interrupt his concentration. You can't hear *him* or *his* directions while *you* are talking. Excessive talk or gossip is always rude.

- Don't ever chew gum in the studio. This is an ugly habit. (Need I mention not to chew tobacco?)

- If you make any sort of mess, be it from food, drink, make-up or hair supplies, clean it up.

- Only use the telephone if absolutely necessary and be sure to ask first. Make your call brief.

- Drugs are absolutely forbidden.

Simple respect, politeness and consideration are essential in a professional model. They make the difference between a short or long-term career.

For me, being professional is always being prepared and respecting the client and their product. I go into each studio as if I'm seeing a new client, whether I've been there before or not. I never get too relaxed. I always bring more than requested. As for the client, if you don't like the clothes, you shut your mouth. Remember that you're getting paid—you're there to do a job, not to socialize.
Michael Colliander
Model

You must treat every go-see and audition as if it's the chance of a lifetime. Even if your cat died the night before, you have to overcome your emotions and put everything you've got into persuading the client that you're just the model they want.
Elsa James
Model

GO-SEES AND AUDITIONS

Go-sees (go and see the client) or auditions are basically just that: you go and see, interview and/or audition with an established or potential client. These opportunities arise in various ways:

- The agency might call a studio to introduce you in a "general" go-see.

- A client may call the agency and ask to catch up on who's new in town.

- A client may call the agency to request a go-see for a specific job he is casting (he is searching for a certain "type" of model).

- A client may call in response to your composite received in the mail from your agency.

- A client may have seen you at a social function and request a professional interview with you and your book.

There are, in fact, many other ways a client meeting can come about. The general idea is that you're making a sales call on the client. After reading the previous information on etiquette you should have a good idea of how to handle yourself. Use those tips and the following information to assist you in the days ahead.

The client interview
Interviews are tough in the beginning, but they'll get much easier with experience.

Arrive on time and dressed as the agency has requested. (You'll have a better chance of getting the job if you walk in looking like the photo they have in mind.) If the agent did not make a suggestion on how to dress, ask her. If she does not know, dress mid-stream—not too high fashion and not too casual.

When you are greeted at the door, smile, say who you are and why you are there. (For example, "Hello, I am Annette Cusick from Elite Chicago. I'm here for the beer audition.")

If you are asked to have a seat, sit down and make yourself comfortable. Sometimes you may not have a place to sit; it is not uncommon at go-sees for there to be many other people waiting. Try to smile at everyone and say hello. (Don't be dismayed if no one responds. Most likely they are as shy or nervous as you are. Remember that shyness can come across as arrogance.) You might start up a quiet conversation with someone. (Be careful here—loud conversation can distract someone trying to

work. Also, no gossip!) Bringing a book or magazine is also acceptable. You should be prepared to wait anywhere from a few seconds to an hour and sometimes longer.

There could be many reasons for the delay in interviewing you. Be patient. If you have another go-see or booking, tell the studio manager very politely. Possibly you'll be allowed in next. If this is the case, apologize to the other people waiting and say thank you. Believe me, it will inevitably happen to them too.

More than likely a client will have seen a lot of people before you and will probably see many after you. You may all have similar physical characteristics. What makes you different from the others? What do you have to offer that they don't? Why should the client book you? Know the

Go-sees are informal interviews with potential clients. Several models may be seen at the same session, so be prepared to wait and take a book or magazine to help pass the time.

DAN ZAITZ

> *Make a list of things to discuss, so you have an agenda once the conversation gets going. Always be direct. Don't waste the client's time or yours.*
>
> Tom Bien
> Model

answers to these questions before you go into any interview. You are there to sell yourself.

When your name is called, stand up and follow the person who addressed you into the interview room. Smile and say hello to the people who are doing the interviewing. Shake hands firmly if you choose to (a limp handshake is a turn-off). State your name and which agency has sent you. Wait for an invitation to sit down. (Some clients will do the interview as you stand. Don't worry—this is not unusual). Be prepared to hand over your book for inspection.

An interview may last from thirty seconds to thirty minutes; you cannot predict how long or short it will be—just flow with it. Normally when you go into an interview, everyone is under pressure to find the right model(s) as quickly as possible, to book them and to produce the rest of the photo session while juggling with the other daily activities. Often a client will have a couple of auditions for different jobs on the same day.

If time allows, take the opportunity to bring out your personality—naturally! You don't have to go into a tap dance or sing—just be yourself. That way the client has a better insight to you and your photos. You know when you click immediately with some social contacts but others take a little longer to warm up to? This is all to do with personal chemistry. Photographers and clients are like that too. Sometimes you'll immediately get along and sometimes it will take longer to warm up to them. Your mood and their mood are factors in determining the success of the interview. Regardless of their behavior, always remain friendly, calm and professional. (Remember you are selling a product—yourself. If you believe in the product then they will also. Sometimes it won't be immediately. Don't push too hard! This is also part of establishing your reputation.)

After your book has been seen and handed back to you, the interview is probably over, depending on the conversation. Leave your composite with the interviewers. If they do not want your composite, don't be hurt. If you're not appropriate for that job, your card will only confuse them when they're trying to decide whom they will book. Stand up, smile and say, "Thank you for your time. It was a pleasure meeting you." Shake hands if you're comfortable doing so and walk out of the room.

Photographers and clients often have incredible memories. They may not book you for that particular job, but they will keep you in mind for the future. It is not uncommon for weeks, even months, to go by before the photographer or client phones the agency and requests to see you again for a new job being cast.

I cannot possibly tell you everything about how to interview on your go-sees or auditions in this chapter. Take the information that you've read and apply it to the situation as you feel appropriate. This book gives only guidelines, not mandatory rules.

ON THE TELEPHONE

Communication is another crucial key to success. When you are calling a place of business do not make it a guessing game as to who you are and why you are calling. Every second you waste is time—and time is money. You'll impress people if you don't waste their time. Say immediately who you are and why you are calling.

I received a phone call one particularly hectic day and the caller said, "Ummm, ughhh, hello. Ummm, ugh, I was walking down the ummm street yesterday with my friend, Sally and ummm ughhh we were looking at the magazine covers and ummmm ughhh I mean Sally said she had an aunt who knew a girl who ummmm ughhh knew a photographer . . ." I said, "Here, maybe I can help. Are you interested in becoming a model?" She said, "Ummm ughhh, yes! How did you know that?" I then explained to the caller how our agency handles new models.

Can you imagine going through several of those conversations a day while trying to take care of a highly pressurized business? I have made appointments with people immediately just because I liked the way they handled themselves on the phone. The telephone call is also part of your sale. If you cannot communicate before you get an interview, I wonder if you'll be able to communicate in the interview itself. If you are nervous, practice with your friends; it may feel silly but you'll learn the habit of preparing yourself for all sorts of telephone conversations.

Try to get on and off the telephone as quickly as possible, but without babbling. Excessive conversation is irritating and unnecessarily distracting. If you are making an inquiry, be ready to write down the information. Don't call people and interrupt their answers to your questions with, "Oh, can you hold on while I find something to write with?" They have many other priorities in their day, so try not to irritate them. Some examples of direct, business-like inquiries are given in Chapter 1. Of course, the more familiar you become with people, the longer the conversation. You needn't become a robot. Just develop good habits when dealing with people who are under a lot of pressure.

SOCIALIZING

Socializing is an integral part of the modeling business. It does help to be seen in the right places, but proceed with caution! If not handled properly, certain types of socializing could have a negative effect on your reputation. Now, here's the tricky part—what is "proper?" Everyone marches to a different drummer and what is proper for you may not be so for others.

Numerous business situations will present themselves: in restaurants, studios, hotel rooms and so on. Who pays the check? Should you drink alcohol or refuse drugs? What should you wear? Should you go off your diet to make a client more comfortable? Should you sleep with a client in order to get a job?

If you have issued the invitation—to lunch, dinner or whatever—you should pay the check. If you've been invited, your host should pay the

BRAD CALCATERRA

check. If it was a mutual decision, each person should pay his or her share. If there is any doubt or discomfort, just ask, "Shall we go Dutch?"

It is not considered unprofessional to have a glass of wine or a cocktail with dinner. Only you know how much alcohol you can handle and a professional would never drink too much while doing business. Listen to yourself.

Drugs are bad for your skin, your mind, your hair, your body and your general health and well-being. They are destructive elements in a professional model's career. If they are offered to you, politely refuse.

What you should wear depends upon the situation. If you are dining at a smart restaurant or going to a formal event, dress up; for a more relaxed atmosphere, dress casually. Be comfortable with yourself and the way you look. Clean and simple is always the best choice. Tattered or dirty garments are entirely unprofessional. Avoid items that are too trendy and do not wear heavy make-up. Always remember that your clothing is an extension of yourself and perceived that way by others. If there is any doubt in your mind, ask your agent what is appropriate.

Parties and social gatherings can present great temptations in the way of food and drink. Don't feel pressured by people offering you cheesecake when you are on a diet. They should understand, and even if they don't, it is not impolite to refuse their offers. Remember, it is possible to have a good time and still watch what you consume.

No matter how old, how experienced or how professional you are, there will always be tricky situations to handle. Whatever your behavior, be aware of it and accept the consequences.

Don't ever have sex with someone who promises you a job in return. Chances are you won't be given the job and you'll simply get a bad name for yourself. Modeling has a promiscuous reputation (not entirely unfounded) but the best rule is always to follow your instinct. Behave professionally and others will respond in kind. Power has a strange way of affecting people. For many it means exerting power over others. I believe it is important to have power over yourself. Let other people worry about themselves. If you don't want to do something, don't do it. If you do want to do something, go ahead. Always keep in mind that your behavior is part of your reputation. How do you want people to remember you?

Apart from being a good way to make useful contacts, socializing is also a great way to relax. But beware getting too relaxed — you don't want to end up saying or doing something you might regret later. Reputations are fragile things.

If you are out socializing and a client doesn't remember you, don't be hurt. There are hundreds of models and it's difficult to remember everyone. Defuse any embarrassment by reintroducing yourself. Don't be surprised if some people pretend not to know you; this happens a lot. I laugh when people do this to me – if it makes them feel more important, who am I to spoil their fun?

Insecurity can also alter people's behavior. Modeling tends to breed insecurity, possibly because the future is always uncertain. Regardless of your environment or what is going on, insecurity can pop up at any time. It's understandable that you may be overwhelmed by some people when you are just beginning your career. The more experienced you are, the more secure you should become.

Photographers, hairdressers, make-up artists, clothing stylists and models are all hired for their abilities to fill the client's job requirements. Sometimes you will succeed, sometimes you won't. Try to keep a positive attitude and treat people as you want them to treat you. Yes, this is an old adage but you'll be amazed how well it works. It's very important to get out there and try. You'll eventually find a system that works for you.

COURTESIES

Acknowledgements of appreciation are not old-fashioned! Something as simple as a card, a rose, a cigar or a basket of fruit, just to say "thank you" to someone special is always appreciated and your thoughtfulness will be remembered. It doesn't have to cost a lot. The small investment you make will come back to you time and again.

If you have made a *faux pas* or mistake you regret, a simple gesture of consideration can easily persuade someone to forgive your foolishness.

Our model, Devin Devasquez, inadvertently double-booked herself to two major clients just as her career was taking off. It was a bad blunder and involved letting one of the clients down—in fact, that client vowed never to use her again.

In this instance, I suggested that Devin send the client some flowers by way of apology. They received no immediate acknowledgement from the client, but several weeks later that same client called me to offer Devin more work, saying that her thoughtful gesture had been appreciated.

If you find yourself in a spot like this, the least you should do is to write a brief letter of apology to the client (in some cases your agent might insist you write the letter in her presence so she can approve it). The form of your apology (letter, flowers or whatever you think appropriate) depends on how well you know the client. Don't be nervous of saying sorry for your mistakes—a graceful apology can work wonders.

DAN ZAITZ

CHAPTER 5

MODELING OPPORTUNITIES (for men and women)

Print opportunities
•
"Live" opportunities

Modeling has opportunities for many different types of model. The group assembled here all make a very good living from their particular markets: Stanley Gluck (character), Amy Vollmer (full-figure), Caralien Miller (petite), Steve Wood (ethnic) and Vicki Kruse (older).

I could have written a book on this subject alone—there is so much for you to know. The first thing to be aware of is that modeling can be broadly divided in two: print work and live work. Within these two areas there are many different opportunities. In this chapter I describe the most commonly available opportunities around the world and give you enough information to decide which area sounds appropriate and feasible for you. Keep in mind that the more involved you become in this industry, the more educated you'll become. As a result you'll be able to make better decisions and have more control over your career.

Three years ago I could have easily broken down modeling into several well-defined categories. Today that is not the case. Every day there are more and more people getting into the business. As a result, there is a constant influx of new talent around the world with new ideas and advertising strategies. They are constantly experimenting and changing the standards. Sometimes the new talent and its ideas are accepted, sometimes not. You must keep up with new developments in the industry in order to compete worldwide. You must also be versatile to give yourself maximum opportunities for work. Remember, there are hundreds of markets to experiment in (each with its own terms and definitions). This chapter deals mainly with fashion modeling.

The term "fashion" refers to clothing and accessories. To work in this area you must be a sample size.

Female

Straight	5ft 8in–5ft 11in	
	Size 6–8: 34B–24–34	
Full-figure	5ft 8in–5ft 10in	
	Size 12–14: 38C–28–39	
Petite	5ft 3in–5ft 6in	
	Size 3–4 or 7–8: 32B–24–34	

Male

5ft 11in–6ft 1in
Size 40R: 15½in neck; 32in waist; 34in inseam.

MICHAEL MARIENTHAL

MICHAEL MARIENTHAL

Advertisers frequently show their garments on attractive people in sophisticated situations — but not simply to show the clothes to advantage. They believe that potential customers like to imagine themselves in similar situations, so these advertisements both inspire and fulfil fantasies.

> " *My advice to models, regardless of their area of interest it to realize who they are—what it is that is special and unique to them—and to capitalize on those attributes.* "
>
> John Welzenbach
> Photographer

Modeling clothes is an art. You must learn how to walk, move and show off the clothing to stimulate the sale. When potential customers look at a model they are generally imagining themselves in that same outfit. Clothing is designed to appeal to those leading specific lifestyles, and to those who simply aspire to them. In this way clothing can both create and fulfil daydreams and status.

The model's image must enhance the image of the clothes and this must be consistent throughout the campaign: the model, the mood, the clothing, the art direction and the advertising placement. Keep in mind that if you do not get a job, your "look" may have been considered inappropriate for that particular shoot. Do not take it personally. Perhaps you will have the right image for the next audition.

Fashion modeling encompasses everything from glossy fashion magazines (editorial) to mail-order catalogues, from live shows for *haute couture* houses to "rag trade" promotions.

PRINT OPPORTUNITIES

Catalogue

This is exactly what the name suggests—photos of specific merchandise, from sweaters to saucepans, presented in a strict style in a catalogue. It is crucial to move gently and slowly in catalogue shots, always keeping the line of the garment in mind. (The garment has normally been pressed, pinned, taped, clamped and sewn into place.) Not surprisingly the models usually look so stiff they resemble store window mannequins. Each photo is accompanied by "copy"—written information about each item on display.

Mail order catalogues were originally aimed at the rural shopper unable to get into town to buy clothes. As home shoppers became more comfortable with the concept of catalogue shopping, their tastes became more sophisticated. As a result the catalogue producers had not only to keep current with fashion, but also produce attractive, up-to-date catalogues. For years now city dwellers have also been using catalogues to do their shopping, so the market has opened up considerably, creating more jobs for the catalogue model.

Within the field of catalogue work, there is a growing need for models who are not of straight size or appearance: full-figure, petite, ethnic and older models. The modeling agency is constantly

101

> ❝ *People are becoming more aware of full-figure models . . . and realizing that we are also beautiful. For me, that's one of the most exciting things. I have become more confident and can handle situations that I wouldn't have been able to before.* ❞
>
> Amy Vollmer
> Full-figure model

Amy Vollmer

Height 5'8½ Dress Size 14 Bust 38 Waist 28 Hips 42 Shoes 10 Hair Blonde Eyes Hazel
Hauteur 1.74 Confection 44 Poitrine 96 Taille 71 Hanches 107 Chaussures 41 Cheveux Blonds Yeux Noisette

PHYLLISS CUINGTON

PHYLLISS CUINGTON

PHYLLISS CUINGTON

big beautiful coats

sale 142.50
A winning shape for women, by Perlette. (left) In warm wool/nylon blend, meticulously tailored with asymmetric closing, diagonal tuck front details and stand-up neckline. The effect is flattering . . . fashionable! Women's sizes 16-22. Made in the U.S.A. Will be $190. (D. 151)

sale $195
Coat fashion for the larger woman, in pure wool with high-voltage color. (right) The jade coat from Presentation by Fashionbilt features a full, European-inspired silhouette with long shawl collar, intricate buttonhole and pocket detail. Brilliant! Women's sizes 16-22. Made in the U.S.A. Will be $260. (D. 151)

For your convenience: Merchandise availability is listed in our Shopping Guide located in the center of this book.

The best coat prices guaranteed. See page 14.

> ❝ *I have to watch my weight. Everyone thinks I can 'pig out' because of my size, but that isn't true.* ❞
>
> Amy Vollmer
> Full-figure model

attempting to fill the needs of its clients. We scout and sign models according to their specifications. When we fill our quota for that type, we move on to the next area of need. If an agency tells you, "We already have a couple of your type," keep in mind that these are specialized areas. Agents are in business to make money. Sometimes we lack diplomacy, so please accept our apology in advance if we are too abrasive. We really do try to be delicate when we say no to a model. If you're sensible, you won't take it personally. Take it as a challenge. Timing is everything. Don't be easily discouraged. Whenever you are among the minority you will inevitably meet competition for those few openings.

Full-figure modeling

This really began in America, but it's slowly creeping into other countries. Two years ago my agency in Chicago did not represent any full-figure models. We now have two and both are earning a very good living. They model exactly the same clothes as straight size models, but in full-figure sizes. I have been at many American conventions where European agents have teased me about scouting for full-figure women. Now some of those agents have begun looking for themselves!

Full-figure modeling tends to attract older women, but agents are particularly on the look-out for young women aged 19–30 who are 5ft 8in–5ft 10in and wear a size 12–14.

> ❝ *We've had models who have gone into a shoot and seen the schedule board reading: '8.00 Two girls from Elite. 10.15 Two girls from Willie. 12.30 The fat ones.' We prepare them for this and tell them they are going to run into people who aren't going to respect what they do.*
>
> *As far as the requirements, I want everything that Elite wants, only in a slightly larger package. I want a girl that is 'drop dead'—and it's not just her face and body – it's her whole presence.*
>
> *The messages came through loud and clear for years—that if you're not tall and young, very beautiful and extremely thin, you're a worthless piece of garbage. That is simply bogus.*
>
> *The first question I ask is, 'How do you feel about your size?'. If anyone feels a little shaky about it, I tell them, 'Think a little longer and call me back.' If we do a composite that says you are size 14, then that is the size you have to be—you can't lose weight.* ❞
>
> Mary Duffy
> Full-figure/petite agent

Petite modeling

While also begun in America for the same reasons as full-figure modeling, petite modeling has been around a lot longer and is growing rapidly in other countries. Unlike full-figure women, who are limited by their size, petite models can also work in part modeling, beauty and as juniors, because these areas don't require height.

You might have heard rumors that small models are paid small rates—not true! They are paid just the same as other fashion models. So if you're 5ft 3in–5ft 6in and are a size 4–6, petite modeling may interest you.

> ❝ *'Petite girls have to try harder because it's a limited market. They're competing against their own size and also the taller models. It should encourage them to know a few things, like: height isn't a requirement for beauty ads, most American designers now have a petite line, and TV is a great area for petites. One advantage is that a lot of leading men aren't six feet tall, so they need smaller women.* ❞
>
> Rosemary Bennett
> Agent

A petite model's comp-card

Ethnic modeling

"Ethnic" usually refers to people of Black, Oriental, Indian or Hispanic origin. The demand for ethnic models is growing tremendously. However, modeling is in a constant state of flux, so don't be disheartened if you don't fit the bill immediately—your turn will come.

Ethnic models work in fashion, full-figure, petite, part, older and product print modeling. If you are one of the ethnic types listed above and are unsure about your suitability for particular markets, consult an agency.

> *Kids wanting to become models should take their education seriously—knowledge is power. Stupid people don't last and they never excel.*
>
> Don Talley
> Model

> *Being mulatto you don't fit into the Black or White category. The White client tries to use Blacks who aren't too ethnic-looking. They are usually interested in lighter skinned and classical type features. Black (minority) clients usually opt for a definite ethnic look so that they appeal to their market. Mulattoes can fit into a variety of jobs ranging from white to black, and will also be cast for jobs as Hispanics. You'll be rejected for jobs that require a specific ethnic type.*
>
> Rita Craig
> Model

> *The Black/petite market has opened up so much – it's amazing. I think there is a petite catalog going out every week in New York now.*
>
> Marita Monet
> Model

MICHAEL ROBERTS

Being an ethnic model does not confine you to working only for ethnic markets. If you are a real professional, you'll be able to get work in all areas of modelling.

> ❝ *Since becoming a model, I take better care of my skin. I love to play basketball—at least three times a week—but I have to be careful about scratches. I feel like a sissy!* ❞
>
> Don Talley
> Model

Height 5'7¼ Dress Size 8 Bust 35 Waist 25 Hips 36 Shoes 9B Hair Light Chestnut Eyes Blue-Green Excellent Legs

1887 CENTENNIAL 1987

Vicki Kruse

An older model's comp-card

Older models

This category is increasingly sought after because there are increasing numbers of elderly people in the world. These people have money to buy products and they want to see themselves represented in advertising. For example, a woman in her forties might not be persuaded by a 20-year-old promoting a hair coloring product; similarly, it is very difficult for a man of 75 to see himself in a business suit modeled by a young man of 25. As a result, older people increasingly promote clothes and products that their generation is interested in.

Older is relative, isn't it? But generally speaking, people above their mid-twenties are "older" in the modeling industry. They are more likely to be "real people" print models (see page 112) rather than to work in fashion. The market need for older people is based upon the population. Product campaigns are designed to appeal to the population of particular communities, so very few teenagers would feature in advertising campaigns targeted at a predominantly retired audience.

> *"I'm always looking for the perfect figure— someone who can adapt to all areas of catalogue—men as well as women. My idea of a professional is someone who moves well. I don't mean posing. It's the ability to change body movements naturally (especially as there are photographers who don't give good direction), being able to interpret and project the mood necessary. They have to be able to do their hair and make-up well. Also, it's crucial that they have a good disposition. Nobody wants to work with an unpleasant person, especially if you're on location for a while."*
>
> Jim Kirchman
> Fashion director

Editorial modeling

The term "editorial" applies to a section in a fashion magazine *and* to a type of photography. Confusion can arise here because you can actually have a catalogue photographed in editorial style. Generally, editorial photography has a much freer style than that used in standard catalogues; it avoids the traditional, mannequin-like poses against a seamless backdrop. This looser style allows much more creative input.

The editorial area in a magazine is a more subtle sales approach than a standard catalogue. The editor of the magazine decides on the photographers, models, clothing, accessories and locations. He or she is familiar with the basic concept, layout, picture quantity and size before the photo session. However, during the photo session the talent involved will most likely influence the basic concept. As a result there is more freedom of movement and expression by everyone.

The art director will often design a spread around finished photographs, utilizing them in a way that will lend the greatest appeal to the page layouts. The copy is less noticeable in editorial. Pick up a fashion magazine and turn to the editorial section. Look at the movement of the models in conjunction with the clothing. Look for the copy. See how small it is. You almost have to search for the designer, store and prices of the garments. Now look at a Sears or Montgomery Ward catalogue. Look at how stiff the models and clothing are in comparison with the magazine. The copy is obvious. You immediately know what the fabric is, the colors the garment comes in and how much it costs.

A major difference between catalogue and editorial work is the time element. Catalogue

changing patterns

This page, black and white rose-patterned jumper, by Martin Kidman, £255, at Joseph Tricot, 16 Sloane St, S.W.1, and branches. Opposite, navy handknitted wool games sweater, about £80, at Paul Smith, 43-44 Floral St, W.C.2; 23 Avery Row, W.1; Nottingham. Black and white wool dog tooth check trousers, £85, at Stephen King, 315 King's Rd, S.W.3. Black leather loafers, £120, at Crolla, 35 Dover St, W.1; Girl, pink cashmere cardigan, by Richard Higgins at Harrods; Gallery 28, 28 Brook St, W.1. Yellow cashmere scarf, £57.50, both at N. Peal, 37 & 71 Burlington Arcade, W.1. Red wool gloves, at Chanel, 36 Old Bond St, W.1; 31 Sloane St, S.W.1. Red wool tights, at Fogal, 36 New Bond St, W.1; 51 Brompton Rd, S.W.3. Black suede pumps with laces, £170, at Manolo Blahnik, 49-51 Old Church St, S.W.2. Silver cuff bracelet, £121, at Argento, 82 Fulham Rd, S.W.3. Girls' hair and make-up, here and overleaf, by Ray Allington for Vidal Sassoon. Sizes, colours, accessories, see Fashion Information

EAMONN J. McCABE

407A Unforgettable—the way you'll look in your Pantagis dance dress. Stretchy puckers hug you through the torso, then the polka dot skirt stands out and stops short. Flirty side bow is lined in red, just for the fun of it. Black/white cotton, made in USA for 4 to 14 and Petite 2 to 12 sizes 144.00(4.50) Miss Magnin Evening Dresses. Petites, too

407B A.J. Bari embodies the spirited style of the younger set in this black/white cotton print bustier party dress with fabric rose. Drop torso, back zip. Short, of course. Sizes 4 to 12. Imported 195.00(4.50) Miss Magnin Evening Dresses

Everything available through mail order but may not be in every store

7

VICTOR SKREBNESKI

The difference between catalogue and editorial work is clearly shown in these two shots. The models on the left are stiffly posed and there is lots of descriptive text underneath their photo. The model on the right looks far more natural, almost as if he's been photographed 'on the run,' and the text is arranged much more discreetly.

sessions are normally produced to very tight deadlines; there are many garments to shoot in a short period of time. In editorial sessions there is generally a little more time allowed for the creative process.

The editorial sections in magazines provide models with prestigious exposure at minimal cost to the publishers. Fees for editorial work are comparatively low, especially for up-market magazines like *Vogue*. However, models (and agents) accept the low rates because the work is so prestigious and the tear sheets are a valuable addition to a model's portfolio—almost a guarantee of future work. Money is the main reason for doing catalogue work. With luck models may get a catalogue or a catalogue section which is photographed in editorial style and pays catalogue rates. This way you get prestige *and* money!

The clever use of accessories and subtle changes in pace show how the same basic outfit can be presented for three different markets: static catalogue style; slight movement for catalogue shot in editorial style; free movement for full editorial style.

> *Editorial is so much more believable. People like to fantasize themselves in more editorial-type situations—skipping, jumping, spinning, whatever— it's a natural movement. Standing straight up with your head cocked to the side and your mouth half open is unnatural. People identify so much more with natural movement.*
>
> *Good editorial models must be able to move well and understand that, although we are shooting in an editorial style, we are first selling clothes. They have to create the mood and attitude necessary, and still be able to show the detail of the clothing. They have to be actors, creating a shot that will make people stop and look and relate. They must be able to put themselves in the shoes of the person that they are trying to reach.*
>
> Ann O'Malley
> Advertising director

> *Even when an ad is shot in editorial style, it's not truly editorial because it is still a controlled piece of work. In an ad you have certain constraints complying with what the client needs you to do.*
>
> Dave Fleishman
> Photographer

MICHAEL MARIENTHAL

Fashion advertising

This is another sales approach, involving photographic advertisements which focus on the clothing. They are similar to catalogue work but they are single, separate shots placed in appropriate magazines. Generally the designer's name is prominent with a list of places that sell his clothes. Advertising fashion shots can be photographed in catalogue style or in an editorial style. Each shoot demands different approaches. The art director and the client decide the image necessary and plan the project accordingly.

Fashion photography began in Europe, and Europe still sets the standard around the world. In the past you could easily pick out these fashion advertisements in American and Japanese publications. Now these markets are becoming more educated about fashion and consumers are responding to the more European editorial approach. In fact, sometimes when you look through magazines it can be hard to tell editorial spreads from a series of fashion ads.

In the US and Canada the rates for fashion ads are the same as for catalogue work. (In the UK the fashion rate is much higher.) The only time fashion modeling overtakes catalogue work is when a model is contracted to work exclusively for one client, such as the Chanel Girl. The client has to pay an exclusivity fee on top of the daily rate to compensate the model and her agent for other work offers they will have to turn down. If you land an exclusive deal, you've really hit the jackpot, especially if the client produces a variety of merchandise—clothes, perfume, jewelry and so on—because each product in the range is open to separate negotiation.

Opposite and right *These two fashion advertisements are shot in editorial style. Even though the selling copy has not yet been added, it is obvious from the styling that both shots are up-market advertisements and would probably be featured in glossy fashion magazines.*

TOM MADAY

111

MODEL

Product print (Real people)

Any person you see promoting a product in a photo, say, Ivory Soap or Jell-O, is a product model. (Of course, fashion is a product, but it is an area of its own.) Think about all the other non-fashion products available and the variety of people used to promote them. The product may need someone who looks like a fashion model, or possibly a short, heavy-set man with a funny, expressive face, or maybe a woman in her forties. The sky is the limit!

I have often suggested to people that they try product print, usually because they do not have the right look for fashion modeling. It's amazing to watch their reactions: they behave as if I have suggested a vacation in the salt mines of Siberia. It is a great pity that so few people understand the importance of product modeling—the exposure it can give *and* the kind of money that can be made.

Unlike fashion modeling, product print offers many other opportunities. You have to use your common sense in approaching it; look really closely at magazine ads and billboards, examine the product and the type of person advertising it.

> 66 'Real people' is an area of modeling that is often unknown to aspiring models. I think it's sad that so many models are sacrificing a very lucrative career because they only want to be fashion models. 99
>
> John Welzenbach
> Photographer

If you resemble that person in look and age, consider photographing yourself in that way.

Many models have two books: one fashion and one product print; both should be prepared with equal care. Be thorough and watch the details. If you are not a fashion model and you wish to pursue product print, the strategy is the same— just change the concept to match your target market.

> 66 [Product print] can be confusing because the term differs from market to market. A model or modeling agency automatically assume that 'product photography' means 'model with product.' To photographers it means 'still photography without models.' 99
>
> John Welzenbach
> Photographer

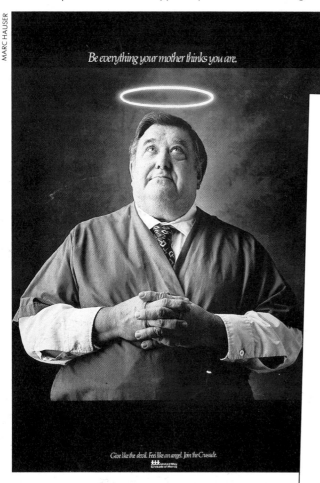

112

Tough clothes for tough customers.

OSHKOSH B'GOSH® UNION MADE IN THE U.S.A.

Part modeling

Widely used in commercial product print, as well as fashion work, part modeling involves separate parts of the body: hands, feet, hair, eyes, teeth, breasts, lips and so on. Some models make an incredible living as part models. Some fashion models do it as an addition to their everyday bookings. Be warned though—part modeling is extremely difficult to stay in, mainly because everything always has to be *perfect*.

It is not unusual for hand models, whose career is literally at their fingertips, to have their hands heavily insured. This is not as silly as it may sound. For example, a cut finger from, say, chopping vegetables could easily result in loss of work and possibly lead to a scar that could permanently damage a career.

I have seen far too many composites with terrible part shots on them. One model had wrinkly hands, dry and flaky skin and her nail polish was chipped. Another model had the focus on her hair which was horribly dry and broken, and sprayed out so far that you could see through

it. This amazes me. Do these people see advertisements photographed like this? Of course not. Please do not pursue this area if you are not "camera ready." This means that the body part has to compete against established models, be in perfect condition and ready to be photographed. Check with your agent and ask to see comps of current part models—this should give you a good idea of the standard of perfection required.

Note that part models in the US and Canada earn exactly the same rate as fashion models: having only part of the body photographed does not mean that part rates are paid. In the UK, the rate is about two-thirds.

Absolute perfection is necessary to be a successful hand model as close-up shots expose the hands to intense scrutiny.

How to appraise your pickle.

This pickle doesn't make the cut. Note the dull color, the soft texture. It's been cooked and stored on grocers' warm shelves.

Here's the real gem. Clearly, a Claussen® pickle. The color is fresh, the texture is crisp. It's never cooked, and always displayed in the refrigerated case. Because Claussen puts an inestimable value on taste.

Claussen.
The upper crunch of pickles.™
Only in your grocer's refrigerated case.
© 1988 Claussen Pickle Co.

DAVE JORDANO

> *Most people don't know just how difficult [part modeling] is. I take a lot of pride in what I do because not everyone can do it. For example, if you're on an all-day shoot, they often expect you to be able to hold a position for up to four or five hours. In TV they expect you to be able to move your hand into the frame at an exact position and move it out time after time after time.*
>
> Brenda Burns
> Part model

> *I have a warning to all the husbands of part models—be prepared to do a lot of housework!*
>
> John Swibes
> Husband of Brenda Burns

Nude modeling

Nude shots are most frequently requested in product advertising and editorial work. The agency will always inform the model in advance and no pressure will be exerted on her to accept. If a photographer and/or client asks you to strip at a shoot without prior warning through your agent, don't do it! Such a request is completely unethical, so phone your agent and get her to deal with the situation. Note that the fee for nude or topless modeling is frequently triple the normal rate.

> *A great model will project a feeling to the camera that will belie her true personality. For example, an ingenue will display sophistication, a wild girl will appear reserved and demure.*
>
> Stan Malinowski
> Photographer

Illustration modeling

Illustration models pose for drawings or renderings wearing clothes, holding a product or perhaps posing for a book cover. Before the days of photography, illustration was the only printed form of fashion advertising. This method is still used occasionally as it is much less expensive than photography. It also gives the illustrator and/or manufacturer the freedom to change the appearance of a garment, and even change the model's face or hairstyle, if they wish. The pay for illustration modeling is comparatively low, but it is still fashion work and can lead you into other areas of modeling.

> *My advice to models, regardless of their area of interest it to realize who they are—what it is that is special and unique to them—and to capitalize on those attributes.*
>
> John Welzenbach
> Photographer

Nude modeling can encompass anything from up-market calendar shots to down-market tabloid newspapers. Never strip for a shot unless it's agreed in advance with your agent.

Runway modeling requires more skill than first appearances suggest. You must be able to walk well and move fluidly along a narrow catwalk, showing the clothes to advantage, but never looking down at your feet. Fashion shows are finely-tuned events—one slip could ruin months of hard work.

"LIVE" OPPORTUNITIES

Runway modeling

Runway work involves modeling clothes in a live fashion show. It is a great way to begin a fashion modeling career as it does not require much money. However, it does require a lot of skill. Runway models must move with the grace of a dancer, project the image required and make people want to buy the clothes. In print you can rely on the lucky split-second photograph to capture a look for you; this is not the case on the runway. There is no room for cheating. This is a form of fashion that you must practice as a dancer practices his or her art. You should take all types of dance class and also practice at home with music in front of a full-length mirror. As they used to advise years ago, practice walking around with a book on your head. Practice changing quickly from tennis shoes and shorts into heels and a sophisticated suit. You may even want to practice with other models at home. *Everyone* needs practice. As designers expand their lines, you have to be able to carry off every type of clothing possible, which means changing clothes and mental attitude very quickly. This will make you very competitive.

Unless you work in a small market, it is difficult to get into runway modeling because it requires so much technique, skill and sense of timing. Added to this, runway models are very territorial and rarely welcome newcomers. However, once you have established yourself as good and dependable you will be readily accepted.

Many photographic models become even more established through runway modeling. Becoming a designer's private model can earn you prestige as well as money. Models who move in a couture designer's circle are known as his or her "cabine." The designer teaches the models exactly how to behave, regardless of the environment, which ensures that the designer's public image is always consistent. The opportunity to work for an *haute couture* house comes about very infrequently, so once in, models guard their positions jealously. Note that runway models tend to be more slender than print fashion models, although the basic sizes are the same.

Runway auditions are quite different from photographic auditions. For a start you must be able to walk well, and few print fashion models can. Clients will expect you to appear dressed in their style of clothing, with appropriate hair, make-up, accessories and attitude. You must really do your homework before you audition for runway modeling. Ask lots of questions until you become familiar with the work and style of various designers. Personality and character are major factors in any sort of modeling, but they are particularly crucial in runway work. That audition is your opportunity to convince clients that you understand their concept, that you will be prepared, able to handle the responsibility of their merchandise and not buckle under pressure. Any mistake you make could lose money for a designer. You must always be aware that a great deal of money and many months of preparation have been invested in a show. The designer needs assurance that you are the right person to make the sale.

Backstage at fashion shows is often a scene of mass hysteria. Even if you are doing a marvelous job your client could end up screaming at you just to release some of the pressure. Remain calm, confident and understanding—that is also part of your job. Once you've worked for the client and established trust on both sides, you could have steady employment for years.

There are two show seasons a year: March (winter fashions) and October (spring fashions). In Paris and Milan they tend to last about seven days; in other cities, four or five days. The shows are "staggered" and usually run in the same order: Spain (mainly for new models), Milan, London, Paris, New York, Tokyo. Note that English shows pay the lowest rates.

Wardrobe is crucial in modeling, particularly in show work where you have a diverse clientele to appeal to. If you don't have a decent wardrobe you may have to borrow a few things until you do. The more work you do, the more clothing you'll get, as designers frequently give away their garments at the end of each season. One of the perks of being a model is that you can also buy designer clothes at wholesale prices. Whether you are wearing the clothing or taking it to a job, you should always be prepared and the garments

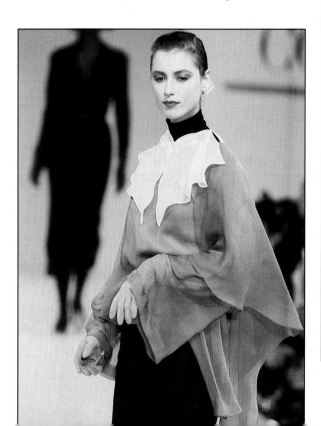

> *One of the biggest problems for new models is lack of clothes. If you're not working regularly, you can't afford to spend much on clothes. On the other hand, you can't keep turning up at interviews in the same old outfits. It helps if you're imaginative and have a sister or boyfriend whose wardrobe you can raid!*
>
> Elsa James
> Model

should be fresh and clean. Even if clients don't request that you bring shoes, stockings and accessories, you'll score extra points if you do. They'll see how professional you are and how much you appreciate the job. Remember that any time you to go an audition or interview you are a sales person. What kind of image do you wish to project? Clothing is the wrapping on that package. Make sure it reflects your intention.

> *Attitude is the key to being a good runway model. You have to 'feel' the garment.*
>
> Tania Cross
> Runway director

Showroom modeling

"Rag trade" manufacturers produce mass-market fashions which they promote within their own showrooms. These shows are very informal and frequently employ very young and inexperienced models, but experience of the runway is very helpful; equally showroom experience is great practice for the runway. Whether modeling lingerie, sportswear, fur coats or formal attire, it's imperative that models know how to move.

In small companies models' duties may also include answering phones and making coffee. In large companies, models may only be expected to model the clothes. The agreement you come to with the manufacturer is individual; you may be employed full-time or simply on a freelance basis as and when shows arise. Manufacturers like live shows as they create a much stronger impact for buyers and/or the press than mannequins, and they can get a real feeling for how the garments move on a human being.

These shows are strategically placed around the changing seasons. Buyers purchase fall and winter lines during the early summer, and spring and summer lines during the fall and winter months. Showroom models are generally busiest around holidays. The money is not especially high but it is steady work and offers many opportunities to build up a network of contacts. You can always supplement your income by pursuing other avenues in modeling.

Informal modeling

An informal model, also called a "trunk show" model, is usually hired to promote a store opening or a new line of clothing for a designer. Such models might be seen in a boutique, shopping mall, at a lunch, or even in a private home. These models must be able to walk well and talk intelligently about the line they are promoting in case the client asks questions, such as, "Is that dress comfortable?"

Some informal models travel for a specific company, others are freelance. Those attached to a company could be involved in a production as big as a choreographed music show.

Promotion modeling

Promotion models are usually freelance and sell products as well as clothing. They are hired a short time in advance by the fashion or public relations directors of department stores. Promotion models are the ones who ask if they can spray you with a "sensational new cologne," or press you to try on "Europe's latest design." The money is relatively low, but it can usefully supplement a new model's income. Promotion modeling is another opportunity that many people ignore, but like anything else in life, you can work it to your advantage.

Fit modeling

A "fit" model is one whose body is exactly the right size for a designer's sample garments. A perfect fit is essential and the model's body size cannot fluctuate even a fraction, as measurements (from shoulder to elbow, from elbow to wrist, and so on) are so precise. Fit models might have to stand for hours and hours as the designer and assistants pin and sew garments to their bodies. Models could spend days watching them piece together a new line and then decide not to continue with the production.

This may not sound like very glamorous work, and perhaps it's not, but it can lead a model into other areas of the industry. He or she may be chosen to do the designer's ads or runway show—anything is possible. Although this type of modeling does not pay a lot and is extremely demanding, it is a valuable education: fit models learn a lot about fabrics, design and construction of clothing which helps them to understand how to work with the garments after their completion.

Convention modeling

This type of modeling is really the most difficult. Convention models are on their feet all day, often in huge, purpose-built convention facilities, selling products they might have seen for the first time only that morning to vast numbers of potential customers. Convention models generally earn more per day than editorial, fit, illustration and

MICHAEL MARIENTHAL

*Promotion and convention modeling may not be your
real ambition when you start out, but both can provide
useful experience of interacting with people and lead to
other opportunities.*

promotion models, but unfortunately, this type of
modeling is the least respected by many people in
the fashion industry—they feel that conventions
are beneath them.

To do convention modeling you need an
attractive face, the ability to answer the same
questions over and over again, a sense of humor,
stamina and the tolerance to smile all day. When
convention models do a good job they are happily
rehired by clients, often many months in advance.
Can you imagine having secure bookings several
months in advance? Few fashion models can
boast the same. So, if you're of strong character,
enjoy public contact and are a great salesperson,
convention modeling could be for you.

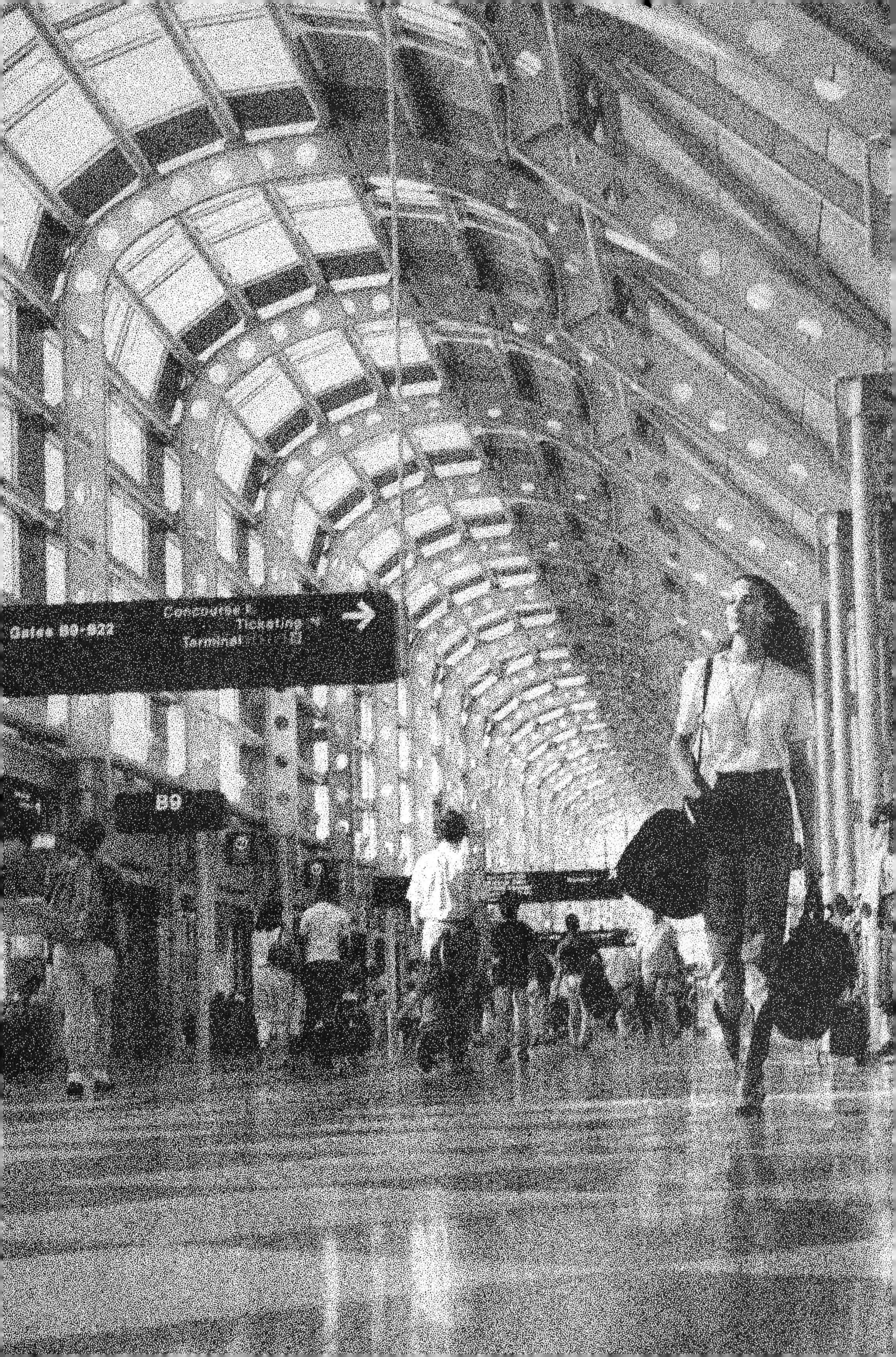
Ticketing
Terminal
B9

J. CORTLAND BOYD

CHAPTER 6

MODELING AROUND THE WORLD

Travel tips
•
Foreign markets

Traveling to new markets will not only enhance
your career, it will also increase your confidence
and open your eyes to different cultures.

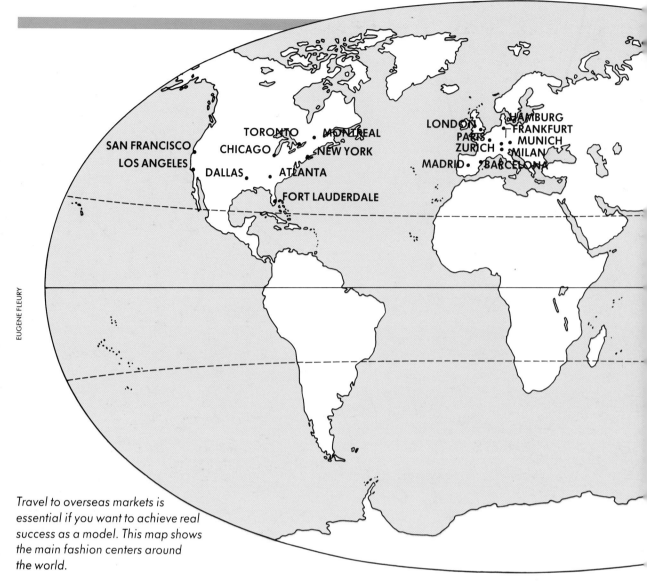

EUGÈNE FLEURY

Travel to overseas markets is essential if you want to achieve real success as a model. This map shows the main fashion centers around the world.

To be a really successful model, you must be prepared to travel outside your home country. Chapter 2 explained why and when you should travel to experience different markets. This chapter is intended to help you understand the various world markets and to make your movement from one city to another much easier.

Imagine this situation: you arrive for the first time, alone and nervous, in Japan. You're a long way from home and you don't speak the language. You have to get from the airport to the center of town, but which way do you go? Where is the taxi rank? Is there a bus service? Every sign you see is written in Japanese. Help!

It can be very disorienting to arrive in a foreign country whose language and culture are quite alien to you. Is it all right to hail a taxi in the street? Should you tip the driver? Is it safe to go out alone after dark? Is English widely spoken? These are just a few of the questions that will inevitably cross your mind—but once again I must stress that the best line of defence is to be prepared. Before you leave your home territory, contact the tourist office of the country you intend to visit and get maps and brochures. While nobody expects you to master every foreign language, you can learn a few

essential words: please, thank you, where is ..., the days of the week and the numbers. The local people will appreciate your making the effort, but most of all, you will feel more confident if you don't have to rely on sign language alone.

I've tried to cover (briefly) everything you'll need to know to have a trouble-free journey, but there is no substitute for first-hand experience. Ask other well-traveled people for their advice; even if they're not models, they can still give lots of useful information.

TRAVEL TIPS

Before you get on the plane

- Telephone the agency at your destination and confirm details of your accommodation. Leave a note of the address and telephone number with family and/or friends in case of emergency.
- Ask the agency how much the taxi fare from the airport should be and whether you should tip the driver. Although taxis are more expensive than public transport, they are convenient and lessen the anxiety of finding your own way.
- If a member of the agency is to meet you on

122

On the plane

Air travel affects different people in different ways. Taking the following items in your hand-baggage may help to lessen any discomfort you might experience.

- Chewing gum will help to "pop" your ears.
- A large, plastic bottle of mineral water will help prevent dehydration.
- An aerosol can of Evian water is very useful to spray on your face to prevent dry skin. Apply a light moisturizer and lip balm if you do experience tightness.
- Wear minimal make-up; your pores have enough to cope with on the plane, so don't overburden them—you might break out.
- Brushing your teeth will help to refresh you during long trips, so take toothpaste, toothbrush and dental floss.
- Eye drops will soothe dry, irritated eyes.
- Remember to carry any medication or vitamins you're taking.
- Keep your passport, visa, camera and any precious jewelry with you. Ideally, try to avoid traveling with anything really valuable.
- Good reading material and/or a personal stereo help to pass the time.
- At the risk of upsetting airlines, I have to say "Avoid airline food." It is high in salt and preservatives which can create water retention, slow digestion and constipation. Take some fresh fruit and vegetables to eat, but ask the airline first.

Jetlag

On long-haul travel (any journey involving a time difference of more than three hours), jetlag can be a big problem. Unfortunately, there's no sure way of dealing with it. Until your body becomes familiar with the effects of jetlag it's difficult to know what to do about it. My best advice is to try and stay awake until the appropriate time to sleep at your destination. If you *must* have a nap on the plane, keep it brief.

At your destination

In these days of high security, many countries have armed guards strolling through their airport terminals. If you've never come across this before, it can be quite intimidating. Don't be concerned—they are there for your protection.

Part of the fun of traveling abroad is seeing how other people live and eating unusual food. But there are several precautions you should take to ensure you stay healthy and able to work efficiently.

- Always drink bottled mineral water and use it for cleaning your teeth. Your whole system can be easily upset by foreign tap water.
- Avoid eating food from street merchants—it's not always hygienically prepared and stored.

arrival at the airport, make sure you have his or her home phone number, or that of the agency owner—just in case.

- Don't overpack! Traveling light will get you in and out of planes and trains with minimum hassle. Also, if your luggage is stolen or lost (it *can* happen), you won't lose too much.
- It's a good idea to wear (and take with you) lots of black clothes. Black can carry you from one occasion to another with a few accessory changes.
- Remember to pack your hairdryer and travel iron, plus electrical converters and/or plugs.
- Have at least $50 (including some coins for telephones) in the currency of the country you are visiting.
- Make sure you get a flight that arrives during daylight hours—it makes it easier (and less intimidating) to find your way into town.
- When making your reservation ask for a seat near the bulkhead (the partition dividing the cabin), or near emergency exits, as these areas usually have more leg-room.
- Allow at least two hours' checking-in time when traveling overseas—it can take ages to get through all the formalities.

FOREIGN MARKETS

The following section has been compiled to help you understand what markets are available to you. It is in no way intended to replace the advice and recommendations of your agent. Information changes all the time as the industry, markets and agencies are constantly changing. Even though I made many phone calls to agencies all over the world and spoke with many experienced models, I found a wide variety of opinions on each topic.

This chapter gives a breakdown of twenty-one different cities and the information under each is divided into the following categories:

Market

It is impossible to outline all the types of modeling you will encounter in each city. I have concentrated mainly on fashion modeling, but each market usually has a little bit of everything. It's up to you to be resourceful—find out what each market has to offer and prepare accordingly. Note that the seasons vary from market to market and may even be different for male and female models. Check these things out when you arrive.

Portfolios

Wherever you go in the world, always send your pictures in advance and place a call to your new market prior to departure. Also take with you all your most flattering and current pictures. Try to include editorial, catalogue and character shots.

Don't assume that you will know what the agent at the other end will like; I've sometimes found photos tucked away in the back of a book which I've liked more than those on display. If your book is weak but your look is strong, you can, of course, put your book together in your desired market, but this will cost more and delay your ability to work.

Composites

Comp-cards are much more problematic than portfolios. A card from Zurich, for example, may work well there, but agents in Italy may insist on having a new card for their market. Similarly, the Italian card may be unacceptable in Los Angeles, so yet another one has to be printed . . . This should not happen a lot—but it *does* happen. Each agent and market may have different approaches. When you have traveled a bit you'll be better able to predict individual requirements.

Wardrobe

The best advice I can give is to wear lots of black: it tends to be the safest foundation for a "look"— but be sure to inquire first.

Travel documents

Obvious as it may sound, make sure you have a *current* passport. Jobs abroad can crop up at very short notice and it can take several weeks for a new passport to be processed. Don't miss out on work opportunities by being ill-prepared.

The visa/working paper situation varies from person to person, so it is very difficult to pin down.

The information I give here applies only to American models and is current at the time of going to press. To be safe, contact the agent at your destination and ask for advice.

Airports
It can be rather unnerving the first time you arrive in a country and have to find your own way to the city center. For this reason I give the names of the major airport(s) serving each city and the approximate time it takes to get into town using taxis and/or public transport. Make sure you have some coins or small denomination notes for paying fares and tipping.

Accommodation
The type and availability of accommodation varies from city to city. If an agency has invited you to come, it will usually arrange some sort of housing. Most agencies have their own apartments which are less expensive to rent than private apartments. While this is convenient, remember that you will probably be sharing with one or more people. (I call it "dormitory life" because the population is so transient.)

If you're not already represented by an agency abroad, chances are that you won't be offered much help in finding accommodation. In this case the best thing to do is ask the advice of a model just returned from the relevant market. If you can't find someone, your agent will be able to help you.

Transport
Most cities have good public transport: subways, buses, taxis, bicycles . . . but there are cities where a car is essential. In the city breakdown, I specify which places this applies to.

Payment and commission
Payment schedules and commissions vary from agency to agency in Europe, while in America they tend to be the same for exclusive talent. Don't forget that some European governments take 20 percent (sometimes 25 percent) of your earnings (less than in America).

Length of stay
How long you stay in a particular city obviously depends on how well you are received, how much you like that market and how much your agent believes in you. If you're doing well, you can extend your stay. If you're unhappy, you must talk to your agent there and plan an alternative strategy.

Expenses
This is a tricky area to advise about as the cost of living varies from place to place. If you're good at handling your money, obviously you'll fare better than those who aren't, but whatever your attitude to finances, do take care until you're working. Once you're reasonably established, you'll make friends who may offer to rent you a room in their apartment and this can be a real money-saver. The sums I quote for expenses include rent. These figures are estimates and intended only to give you some idea of what to expect.

125

AUSTRALIA

Melbourne

Market Editorial with more catalogue. Consistent throughout year; slow in January, February and December. Limited minority market. Runway peaks in January and February.
Portfolio/composite Variety of images.
Wardrobe Neat, clean, fashionable; minimal make-up.
Documents Visa necessary.
Airport Tullamarine—about 20–30 minutes from city center by taxi or bus.
Accommodation $70 per week.
Transport Public.
Payment Every 2 weeks.
Commission 20%
Length of stay 2 months minimum.
Expenses $1000 per month.

Sydney

Market Editorial and catalogue. Work consistent throughout year, but relatively slow in January, February and December. Limited minority market. Runway peaks from end January to end May.
Portfolio/composite Variety of editorial and catalogue.
Wardrobe Neat, clean, fashionable; natural make-up.
Documents Visa necessary.
Airport Mascot—about 20–30 minutes from city center by bus or taxi.
Accommodation $70 per week.
Transport Public.
Payment 1st of the month.
Commission 20%
Length of stay 2 months minimum.
Expenses $1000 per month.

CANADA

Montreal, Quebec

Market Editorial with some catalogue. Peaks April, May, September and October. Limited minority market. Runway peaks March, May, August and September.
Portfolio/composite Editorial.
Wardrobe Clean, simple, fashionable.
Documents Visa unnecessary.
Airports Mirabel—about 40 minutes from city center by regular bus service; about 30 minutes by taxi.
Dorval—about 40 minutes from city center by regular bus service, slightly less by taxi.
Accommodation $140–$175 per week.
Transport Public.
Payment Once a month.
Commission 15–20%
Length of stay One month minimum.
Expenses $1000 per month.

Toronto, Ontario

Market Catalogue and editorial. Peaks March, May and October. Slow during January, November and December. Limited minority market. Runway peaks end of October.
Portfolio/composite Editorial with smiles.
Wardrobe Casual, neat, fashionable; little make-up.
Documents Visa unnecessary.
Airport Lester Pearson—about 40 minutes from city center by regular bus service, slightly less by taxi.
Accommodation $100–$140 per week.
Transport Public.
Payment 1st and 15th of month; some pay only once a month.
Commission 20%
Length of stay One month minimum.
Expenses $1000 per month.

FRANCE

Paris

Market Primarily editorial with some catalogue. Busy year round, except August (all agencies close) and December. Limited minority market, except for runway. Haute couture January and July; prêt-à-porter March, September and October.
Portfolio/composite Editorial suggested.
Wardrobe Neat and fashionable.
Documents Visa necessary.
Airports/Aéroports Charles de Gaulle—about 40 minutes from city center (Porte Maillot) by bus or train (Gare du Nord).
Orly—about 30 minutes by bus from city terminal at Invalides, or 20 minutes by train from Quai d'Orsay, Saint-Michel or Austerlitz stations.
Accommodation $140–$200 per week.
Transport Public.
Payment Varies.
Commission 25%
Length of stay 2–3 months minimum.
Expenses $1000 per month.

GERMANY

Hamburg

Market Editorial and catalogue. Peaks mid-March until mid-May, June and September. Limited minority market. Very little runway.
Portfolio/composite Editorial with smiles.
Wardrobe Casual, fashionable; little make-up.
Documents Visa necessary.
Airport/Flughafen Fuhlsbuttel—about 30 minutes from city center by bus to Ohlsdorf station and then train, or 20 minutes by taxi.
Accommodation $140 per week.
Transport Public.
Payment Once a month.
Commission 20%

Length of stay 2–3 months minimum.
Expenses $1200 per month.

Munich

Market Mostly catalogue with some editorial. Peaks January, March and April. August very slow. Limited minority market. Very little runway.
Portfolio/composite Editorial with smiles.
Wardrobe Young, fresh, with some make-up.
Documents Visa necessary.
Airport/Flughafen Riem—about 20 minutes from the city center; buses go to main railway station.
Accommodation $200 per week.
Transport Public.
Payment Once a month.
Commission 20%
Length of stay 2–3 months minimum.
Expenses $1400 per month.

ITALY

Milan

Market Editorial with some catalogue. Busy year round, except August (all agencies close) and December. Peak months are March, April, May and June. Minority market for runway, but otherwise limited. Shows peak mid-February to mid-March and mid-September to December.
Portfolio/composite Editorial.
Wardrobe Casual, fashionable and natural.
Documents Visa unnecessary.
Airports/Aeroporto Linate—about 15 minutes by bus to the city's central station.
Malpensa—about 40 minutes by bus to the city's central station.
Accommodation $175–$200 per week.
Transport Public.
Payment Varies.
Commission 25%
Length of stay 2–3 months minimum.
Expenses $1000 per month.

JAPAN

Osaka

Market Catalogue; little editorial. Peaks May and June. Limited minority market. Little runway.
Portfolio/composite Editorial and catalogue.
Wardrobe Very dressy with make-up.
Documents Visa necessary. Unique situation in that the Japanese agency must invite the model to its market. It then sends a visa application to the model, who fills it out, takes it to the nearest Japanese consulate and obtains a visa.
Airports Osaka International—about 30 minutes by taxi to city center (Osaka Station). Frequent buses and trains, but get someone from the agency to meet you on your first trip.
Haneda—handles domestic flights.
Accommodation Agency provides apartment and

advances cost to model—about $350 per week.
Transport Agency rep drives models to first go-sees and auditions. Thereafter, they must rely on public transport.
Payment Prior to departure, minus any advances for air fare, apartment and allowances.
Commission 40–50%
Length of stay 2 months minimum.
Expenses Take little money; agencies provide an allowance (deducted from final payment).

Tokyo

Market Editorial and catalogue. Slow during January and December. Limited minority market. Runway peaks in April and October.
Portfolio/composite Editorial.
Wardrobe Very dressy with make-up.
Documents Visa necessary. Unique situation in that the Japanese agency must invite the model to its market. It then sends a visa application to the model, who fills it out, takes it to the nearest Japanese consulate and obtains a visa.
Airport New Tokyo International (formerly Narita)—about 90 minutes to city center by taxi or bus, but get someone from the agency to meet you on your first trip.
Accommodation Agency provides apartment and advances cost to model—about $350 per week.
Transport Agency rep drives models to first go-sees and auditions. Thereafter, they must rely on public transport.
Payment Prior to departure, minus any advances for air fare, apartment and allowances.
Commission 40–50%
Length of stay 2 months minimum.
Expenses Take little money; agencies provide an allowance (deducted from final payment).

SPAIN

Barcelona

Market Catalogue. Peak months February and September. Limited minority market. Runway peaks January and February.
Portfolio/composite Editorial with smiles.
Wardrobe Neat, clean, casual, fashionable.
Documents Visa necessary.
Airport Muntadas—about 30 minutes by regular bus to center (Sants Station).
Accommodation $100–$120 per week.
Transport Public.
Payment 1st and 15th of the month.
Commission 20%
Length of stay One month minimum.
Expenses $1000 per month.

Madrid

Market Editorial with some catalogue. Peaks in February, March and April. Slowest during May and June. Limited minority market. Runway peaks

MODEL

in January and February.
Portfolio/composite Editorial and catalogue.
Wardrobe Neat, clean and fashionable.
Documents Visa unnecessary.
Airport Barajas—about 30 minutes by regular bus from underground terminal at Place de Colon.
Accommodation $100–$120 per week.
Transport Public.
Payment 1st and 15th of each month.
Commission 20%
Length of stay One month minimum.
Expenses $1000 per month.

SWITZERLAND
Zurich
Market Editorial, mostly catalogue. Peaks March, end August and end November. Limited minority market. Runway peaks March and September.
Portfolio/composite Editorial.
Wardrobe Neat, clean and casual.
Documents Visa necessary.
Airport Kloten—about 10 minutes from the city center by bus, train or taxi.
Accommodation $140 per week.
Transport Public.
Payment Varies.
Commission 25%
Length of stay One month minimum.
Expenses $1000 per month.

UNITED KINGDOM
London
Market Primarily editorial with some catalogue. Peaks January and March. Limited minority market. Runway peaks February, March and October.
Portfolio/composite Editorial.
Wardrobe Casual, fashionable; little make-up.
Documents Visa necessary.
Airports Heathrow—about one hour from city center (Piccadilly Circus) by subway or bus. Gatwick—about one hour from center (Victoria Station) by train.
Accommodation $100–$150 per week.
Transport Public.
Payment Varies.
Commission 20%
Length of stay 2 months minimum.
Expenses $1000 per month.

UNITED STATES
Atlanta, Georgia
Market Catalogue and a little editorial. Consistent, but slow in December and January. Good minority market. Runway in March, April, September and October.
Portfolio/composite Editorial and catalogue.

Wardrobe Neat, clean, casual; some make-up.
Documents None necessary.
Airport Hartsfield—about 35 minutes from city center by shuttle bus, express bus or taxi.
Accommodation $100–$150 per week.
Transport Car necessary.
Payment Weekly, or on 1st and 15th of month.
Commission 20%
Length of stay One month minimum.
Expenses $1000 per month.

Chicago, Illinois
Market Catalogue with a little editorial. Peaks February to April and July to October. Slow during May, June, November and January. Good minority market. Runway peaks March, May, August and November.
Portfolio/composite Catalogue with some editorial.
Wardrobe Casual and up-market.
Documents None necessary.
Airports O'Hare International—about 25 minutes from city center by taxi, and about 45 minutes by subway (el line) or bus.
Midway—(mainly domestic flights) about 30 minutes from city center by subway, bus or taxi.
Accommodation $150 per week.
Transport Public.
Payment Weekly.
Commission 20%
Length of stay One month minimum.
Expenses $1000 per month.

Dallas, Texas
Market Catalogue. Consistent, but slow April, May and most of summer. Limited minority market. Runway peaks January, March, May, September and October.
Portfolio/composite Catalogue with some editorial.
Wardrobe Dressy with make-up.
Documents None necessary.
Airport Dallas-Fort Worth—about one hour from center by shuttle bus (Surtran); about 30 minutes by taxi to central bus terminal.
Accommodation $150–$175 per week.
Transport Car necessary.
Payment Weekly.
Commission 20%
Length of stay 2–3 months minimum.
Expenses $1000 per month.

Fort Lauderdale, Florida
Market Editorial and catalogue. Peaks October. Limited minority market.
Portfolio/composite Editorial.
Wardrobe Casual and fashionable; natural make-up.
Documents None necessary.
Airport Hollywood International—about 30

minutes by regular bus, slightly less by taxi.
Accommodation $150 per week.
Transport Car necessary.
Payment Weekly.
Commission 20%
Length of stay 1–2 months minimum.
Expenses $1000 per month.

Los Angeles, California

Market Editorial and catalogue. Busy through year, but dead in December. Good minority market. Runway peaks March, April, May, September and October.
Portfolio/composite Editorial with smiles.
Wardrobe Casually, fashionable; natural make-up.
Documents None necessary.
Airport Los Angeles International—about 30–60 minutes from city center by shuttle bus or taxi.
Accommodation $200 per week.
Transport Car necessary.
Payment Weekly.
Commission 20%
Length of stay 1–2 months minimum.
Expenses $1500 per month.

New York

Market Editorial and catalogue. Peaks April, May—August, September and October. Good minority market. Runway peaks April, May, September and October.
Portfolio/composite Variety of images.
Wardrobe Casual, neat and fashionable.

Documents None necessary.
Airports John F. Kennedy (JFK)—mini-bus or taxi to center (Grand Central Station) takes about one hour.
La Guardia—handles mainly domestic flights. About 30 minutes by bus to Grand Central Station. Newark, New Jersey—not as far away as it sounds. Takes about 45 minutes by bus to terminal on 8th Avenue and West 41st Street.
Accommodation $150 per week.
Transport Public.
Payment Once a month.
Commission 20%
Length of stay 2–3 months minimum.
Expenses $1200 per month.

San Francisco, California

Market Catalogue and editorial. Peaks February. Slow in September. Limited minority market. Runway peaks February, April and August. Slow June and July.
Portfolio/composite Editorial and catalogue.
Wardrobe Slightly dressy, with some make-up.
Documents None necessary.
Airport San Francisco International—30–60 minutes to center by Express Airporter bus; slightly less by taxi.
Accommodation $175 per week.
Transport Public.
Payment 1st and 15th of month.
Commission 20%
Length of stay One month minimum.
Expenses $1200 per month.

129

CHAPTER 7

ROLES AND TASKS WITHIN THE INDUSTRY

Agency
•
Photographic studio
•
Modeling schools

The world of modeling involves people in
many different capacities. The important
thing to remember is that all contribute to
each other's success. The key word in
modeling is "teamwork."

DAN ZAITZ

131

You must be aware by now that I love my job, but believe me, there are times when being an agent can be a thankless task. Most people are unaware of the pressures that agents are under, the responsibilities we have, the sacrifices we make and just how much we are misjudged. Can you imagine being responsible for someone else's career, as well as your own? What about being responsible for several other careers, as well as your own?

Everything we do as agents affects our models' careers. We try with all our might to make sure the results are positive, but once in a while we make mistakes—and you should see the response! When we are making the models money and their schedules are busy, we're their best friends. They are happy and complimentary. Then, when there is a slight lull in the market, we promptly become the enemy and are held solely responsible for their schedules slowing down. Models never think that they too could be responsible, perhaps by being overweight, having skin problems, continually showing up late for bookings without their wardrobe, and so on. They're sure the agent is the only reason for their lack of bookings.

---

66 It's a tough business requiring enormous discipline. Imagine weeks of rejection—Monday morning comes with nothing scheduled. It would be much more comfortable to sleep until ten or eleven, but you have to get out there for your seven o'clock run, be at your agency by nine and bug that booker to set up appointments ... 99

Stan Malinowski
Photographer

Modeling is a short-life career. It attracts young people who are given glamor, exposure and rich rewards and these things can go straight to their heads. Success and maturity do not necessarily walk hand-in-hand and it's not unusual for models to turn against an agent who has nurtured their career and been instrumental in their success. As you might imagine, this is pretty upsetting for us. After working in the agency all day, taking clients to dinner, going to photo exhibits, socializing at parties, tracking down irresponsible models until late hours of the night, giving them a bed to sleep in, and expending our energies entirely on models' behalf, we really don't have much time to ourselves. As a matter of fact, private social life is non-existent. Everything we do somehow involves models or clients.

When I leave my environment I forget that people don't know what I do for a living and I frequently receive strange reactions. It's hard not to stare at attractive young men and women, appraising their appearance and wondering if they would make successful models. But other people have frequently misunderstood my interest and thought it must be sexual.

Every agent has many battle stories to tell, as well as the fairy tales. If you want to get a little personal insight to their lives, ask—that's if you really want to hear the truth!

---

66 [Agenting] is a job where you can't make any mistakes—careers are on the line. Models tend to rely too much on agents. We can get them the first booking, but then the models have to be professional enough to get themselves rebooked. 99

Cynthia Joho
Agent

AGENCY

The staff of a modeling agency can be many and varied: agents, bookers, administrators, secretaries, bookkeepers. Administrators generally "manage" the office. The agent and/or booker generally "manage" the models' schedules. The scout is a talent-hunter who travels around the world looking for new talent and placing existing talent. This job is often held by a senior member of the agency and is considered to be a "perk" of long and dedicated service.

It's fascinating to watch a large, busy agency. If you're not in the business it can look like a mad house. A well-run agency functions like a well-oiled machine—it just *seems* like a crazy environment. It's like driving down a country road on a Sunday afternoon and then hitting a big city ramp; if you don't know how to merge with the traffic you can sit for hours waiting for attention.

When I began with Stewart Talent five years ago my position title was "female booker." I answered the telephones, wrote and typed my own correspondence, edited all the female film, laid out all the portfolios, interviewed all the aspiring models, photographers, make-up artists, hairdressers and clothing stylists, scheduled all the female models', hairdressers' and make-up artists' appointments, arranged their tests, cleaned the office ... I was a jack of all trades, filling the roles of administrator, agent, scout and booker. It was not uncommon for me to leave the office at 10.00 P.M. In fact, it was easier to finish my work after hours, when I wasn't dealing with moment-to-moment emergencies.

Jane merged with John Casablancas the year after I started and formed Elite Chicago. Now, as vice-president of that organization, I don't answer the telephones (our receptionist gets angry), or clean the office—but I do my own correspondence, still edit a great deal of the film, lay out portfolios (mainly just for New Faces), interview aspiring models and photographers, arrange a few rounds once in a while and help out with portfolio photography. The rest of the time I am training my new assistant, who will eventually take over the New Faces Division, researching and bidding for more efficient services for the agency, helping the president, Jane Stewart, making collection calls, trouble-shooting, developing and organizing special projects for the agency, and scouting around the world. I call myself the "Mikey" of the office: if no one has time to do something, I try to take care of it.

The Elite staff now consists of a receptionist, three female bookers, one female New Faces booker, two male bookers, one hair, make-up and clothing stylist booker, one runway booker, three bookkeepers, Jane Stewart and myself. Despite this, it still seems as if we need more staff! Although we each have separate responsibilities, we all work together as a team. It is not unusual on a hectic day for Jane to help out the bookers. Regardless of our job titles, we are all sales staff and intermediaries for the models. There is no job too small when you work for an agency.

PHOTOGRAPHIC STUDIO

Each professional has an individual style. As you learn more about the different types of model and the various markets, you will also learn more about the different types of professional and their styles. They all work together. The key is to find the people who have the right style for you and also appreciate your look.

Just as every person has a unique personality, so he or she also has different degrees of talent, different business ethics and practices. It is difficult to describe the "typical" photographer, studio manager, photo assistant, photo rep, hairdresser, make-up artist, clothing stylist or art director. Some people have never had any formal training. They began by picking a career, jumping in and learning by trial and error. Some may start with a little school training, others may have a college degree.

Talent does not necessarily make a person successful. Politics also has a significant influence in our industry, just like any other. I know of many talented people who do not work often; I also know of people who are not considered to be talented who work a lot. Studios can be hotbeds of intrigue, so never gossip or be indiscreet. Even casual remarks, such as, "I went to a really good party last night," will be reported back and used against you if anything goes wrong. Those shadows under your eyes in the finished photograph may be the photographer's fault, but the blame will be laid at your door if you talk freely about your outside activities.

Try to feel positive about working with your chosen professionals, particularly at the beginning of your career. They should talk you through the photo session, explaining every step so that you understand what is required of you for that specific job. If you are uncomfortable or dislike any of them, those feelings will be read on the film.

Some people are extremely difficult to understand. Don't be alarmed—there is considerable responsibility resting on their shoulders to produce a first-rate product. For example, you might begin your day with a nit-picking, highly-strung, over-sensitive photographer who by the end of the day will be low-key, carefree and prepared to compromise. It is important that you try to understand the pressure these people are under. Don't label them or lump them into any kind of category—they are all different, just as models are. And always remember: the more effort you make, the better the relationship you will have with your co-workers, and the smoother your transition from "aspiring" to "professional" model will be.

In many ways the photo studio functions like a modeling agency. Each member of staff, regardless of number, works together as a team. There are studios which have one person acting as studio manager, photo assistant, and "gofer;" other places may have different people in each of those positions. I don't believe models truly understand the pressures, responsibilities and power that each position has to handle. The following breakdown is to give you insight.

Photographer

The photographer is instrumental in developing a model's look. Certain photographers have the ability to see a special quality in a model which may have been overlooked by others. It is the photographer's responsibility to capture the model's unique presence on film. Photography is an art form: the photographer is the artist, the model is the subject and the film is the canvas.

Have you ever visited an art museum? Perhaps you have noticed that what some people admire you absolutely hate—and vice versa. Viewing

> *Friends have sent girls my way who they thought would be wonderful models. Often they are highly attractive, but most lack that indefinable quality which distinguishes a great model from the common. Of course, these girls become confused and disappointed when they see a seemingly less attractive girl move past them to the pinnacle of modeling success.*
>
> Stan Malinowski
> Photographer

pictures is a subjective exercise and no two people will have exactly the same opinion. This is precisely what happens with models. Some people will appreciate your look and some will not. You must try to look at yourself unemotionally and judge your photographs as a whole. It is very difficult at the beginning of your career to distinguish between good and bad photography. Until you develop an "eye" you should rely on your agent's suggestions.

Studio manager

As a studio manager I learned a great deal about the industry and was constantly amazed at just how unappreciative most people were of the position I held.

The first model interview I had was a perfect example of what was yet to come. Stan was out of town and I was alone. I was really nervous and excited. I answered the door and introduced myself to the model. She walked in and said, "Where's Stan?" I said, "Oh, he's out of town; you'll be interviewing with me." "No, I won't," she said, "I don't interview with secretaries!" She then turned around and flung her long hair into my face. She never could figure out why she never worked for our studio.

Another unpleasant experience concerned one of our models, who was waiting in the lobby of a building for the elevator. When the doors opened she walked in. A voice down the lobby yelled, "Please hold the elevator." As the woman ran towards the doors, they closed in her face—but not before she got a look at the model inside who had not held the door for her. The model rushed into the studio because she was late for her call-back, but had to wait a while as there were a few others already waiting. When the model finally got into the call-back, guess who the studio manager was? None other than the woman from the lobby. Needless to say the model did not get the job, but I did get a phone call from the studio manager who didn't mind telling me just what she thought about the inconsiderate model. The model's excuse was that she was late and she didn't want to waste another second, but her haste meant that she was never booked through that studio.

It is so frustrating sometimes when you take a shoot seriously—working so hard, putting in so much time and energy to ensure that the end product is absolutely incredible—when someone you've hired comes in with a bad attitude and doesn't care about the product or you. It makes such a difference when you're working with a professional who takes their work and yours seriously.

Linda Thompsen
Studio manager

The moral of these two stories is the same: be very careful how you treat people. What goes around comes around.

The studio manager is normally responsible for the organization of the studio and all photo session production. The photographer relies heavily on the studio manager. There is no specific training necessary for this job, although a familiarity with photography can be very helpful. The most crucial qualifications are to know how to juggle a lot of people and cope with pressure while keeping cool. The studio manager is an employee of the photographer or studio.

Photographer's assistant

The photo assistant is responsible for anything involving camera equipment. The basic qualification for the job is a good knowledge of photography. (Do you remember the character, Radar, on the TV program, *Mash*? Remember how he was there at the Colonel's side before the Colonel even knew he needed him? Well, that's exactly how a good photo assistant should be.) The assistant rarely leaves the photographer's side. If he does, he returns before the photographer misses him. An assistant can be an employee of the photographer or studio, or may operate on a freelance basis. This position is usually the lowest paid of any in the photo business.

Make-up artist

Studio make-up artists are responsible for making up the models. They may be qualified beauticians or simply have a natural flair for make-up and skin care. They can be employees of the photographer or studio, represented by an agency or freelance. (See Chapter 3 for more information on make-up.)

Hairdresser

The studio hairdresser is responsible for styling models' hair. He or she will normally be trained in cutting, coloring, perming and all the other necessary techniques, and can give the new model good advice on hair care outside the studio. The hairdresser can be an employee of the photographer or studio, represented by an agency, or freelance. (See Chapter 3 for more information about hair.)

Clothing stylist

As the title suggests, the stylist is responsible for the clothing at a photo session. This person will prepare the clothing provided by the client,

A photo shoot is normally a hive of activity, with each member of the team collaborating to produce the best possible photos. Here you can see two male models with the clothing stylist, photographer and art director.

MICHAEL JOSEPH

Above *Before a shoot, the art director prepares a layout to show the photography team how the product should be presented. It also indicates how much space should be left for headings, captions and artwork.* Right *The finished advertisement—a perfect reproduction of the original layout.*

ironing it and sewing buttons and hems if necessary. She also scouts for clothing, accessories and props that will enhance a photo session. The stylist is responsible for acquiring the items, maintaining their condition and returning them to their proper place. Stylists are often clothing designers. While a knowledge of photography can be helpful, it is most important to have a great sense of fashion, the ability to move quickly and work very long hours (before and after each photo session, as well as during it). The stylist can be an employee of the photographer or studio, represented by an agency or freelance.

> *Many times I have preconceived ideas as to how I'm going to style a specific model. Then they walk into the room and their disposition, gestures, body movement and stance will often give me a different direction to go in.*
>
> Lee Ann Perry
> Clothing stylist

> *The photo session is teamwork. If everybody knows their job responsibilities and that they sometimes overlap, it makes everything run more smoothly.*
>
> Lee Ann Perry
> Clothing stylist

Photographer's representative

A photo rep represents the photographer in much the same way as a modeling agent represents a model: he or she sells the photographer's services. The rep must have a knowledge of photography and the photographer's capabilities, and be a good hustler. Reps frequently hold go-sees on the photographer's behalf, making a preliminary selection of faces from which the photographer will make a shortlist. This saves time and keeps a busy photographer up to date with new faces on the market. Most reps are freelance and represent more than one photographer, which means they deal with many different areas of photography. They normally take a percentage from each job they get the photographer. A rep can also be an employee of the photographer and represent only him. In such a case, the rep would also usually act as studio manager.

> 66 *Photo reps are front runners for photographers …looking for more work before the last job has finished …* 99
>
> Roy Skillicorn
> Photographer's rep

Art director

This person can be of vital importance to models, as the art director is the client—the person employing the photographer and all the staff involved in a shoot. Some art directors are freelance, but most work for a specific store or advertising agency. In retail work an art director could be working on six projects in an hour; in advertising work the pace is generally slower—perhaps one project over six months. The art director has to be highly creative while also being responsible for production of the shoot, staying within the budget, meeting the deadline, satisfying his employers and keeping the buyers and their bosses happy.

The art director is the person who conceives the idea, books the photographer and other people involved in the photo session, and art directs the shoot. Back at the office, he then produces the advertisement. In fashion advertising this means the page is laid out (designed), copy (text) is written and typeset, photos are sized, keylining is organized and finished. When the art director approves, the page is sent for the buyer's approval. Finally the ad goes to press.

If the ad is not approved, there have to be reshoots. There could be many reasons for this: maybe the visual presentation doesn't show the merchandise favorably; it could even be that the store has sold out of the merchandise. If reshoots are necessary, it reflects badly on the art director—more expense will be incurred and going over the budget puts his or her job in jeopardy. Is it any wonder that art directors tend to be anxious at photo sessions?

> 66 *Never be pretentious or inconsiderate, and always remember that there is a fine line between being grateful and being ingratiating.* 99
>
> Jim Streacker
> Senior art director

MODELING SCHOOLS
(Personal development)

You will hear many conflicting opinions about modeling schools, but I feel they *can* be of incredible assistance to the aspiring model. At the John Casablancas Modeling and Career Development Center in Chicago, where I teach the final class, many students have no previous modeling experience, while others may have graduated from a variety of modeling schools. Whatever their background, I make sure they have two hours of undivided attention discussing the honest realities of the industry.

Most cities have some type of modeling school or training center; some are independent and some are franchises (run under the auspices of an established modeling agency). Size and/or reputation are not necessarily the best criteria for judging a school. Each school has its own staff, and inevitably the standard varies from city to city. Some of the large franchises have quality control people who travel around monitoring the various facilities. The independent schools generally have no governing body.

If you are interested in self-development, you should visit the various schools or centers and examine what each has to offer. Is everything old and tattered with outdated model photos on the wall? Listen to what people are saying. Are they discussing last year's fashion news? Ask questions. How many successful models have they started? Where did they learn their trade? Did they ever model? Do they help you find a good agency? (Some schools have their own agencies. Sometimes the schools are better than the agency and vice versa.) Do they promise to make you a star? Take that with a grain of salt—there are no guarantees in life.

There are many excellent schools and centers, and there are many bad ones. As a beginner, how can you sort the wheat from the chaff? Do your research! Ask around various agencies, models and photographers. Be prepared for most people to tell you, "Don't spend the money—learn as you go along." This infuriates me! I have the majority of my New Faces take private classes at the John Casablancas Center. They learn about make-up, hair, runway modeling, photo movement and commercial acting. This provides a sound basis on which I can build to make them more competitive. Within a few weeks they learn the basic skills necessary to become a model. At the same time, with my guidance, they work on compiling a portfolio and composite. This means that, after a surprisingly short time, they're nearly ready to go after the big jobs. Remember, clients want models who know what they're doing; they won't waste valuable time waiting for a new model to get it together at their expense.

My classes gave me excellent reference and research for this book. I pack a lot into those two hours, but there's no way I can cover everything my students will eventually need to know. Books can fill the gaps, but I believe the classroom experience is invaluable. It allows you to learn first-hand from experts and you can share your experiences with your fellow students. Everyone develops at a different speed. The classroom can help you to learn from others; you're not there to compete—that should only happen outside the classroom. It is vital to learn all you can so that when you do become a professional model you know your business.

Just like everything else in life, modeling school is an experience from which you get what you put in. Being a student at a good school provides an excellent opportunity to practice your professional habits: being on time, following through on tasks, learning to interact with different people, and so on. The teachers should be demanding, allowing you little margin for error. You need time to concentrate on your development. If you have areas that really need work, the school staff will work along with you, but you have to go in with the right attitude.

A good school will also provide you with access to established agencies around the world. The director of the school frequently acts as a scout for bigger markets. The better the scout's "eye," the more attention established agents will give the school. If a director is known for wasting our time, word will spread not to bother visiting his or her establishment. Conversely, if a director has reliable judgement, we will make a point of visiting the school. It's common sense—we go where the talent is found.

I have had heated discussions with many agents on one issue: they feel that modeling schools should have tougher screening procedures for aspiring models and tell those who don't have potential to pursue other careers. They also claim that unscrupulous schools put the idea of modeling into the heads of people who would never otherwise have considered it. I sincerely believe that, other than yourself, only God knows if you have the potential to do something. Be prepared to hear opinions that differ from your own, and never lose heart. I have taken on lots of models nobody else believed in and they have gone on to become very successful.

Three years ago a beautiful young woman came to me after being turned down by the agencies in New York. I knew why she had been rejected—she was packaging herself all wrong. I had her lose weight and wash off all the make-up. In fact, her portfolio photographs were later taken with almost no make-up. She became very successful in Chicago very quickly. She has now returned to New York and is working for such

prestigious magazines as *Vogue* and *Harper's Bazaar*. Not bad for a young woman who was rejected but didn't give up . . .

When I started Cindy Crawford five years ago there were many photographers who wouldn't shoot her because of the beauty mark on her face. She had also been told by a leading agent that she wouldn't work until she had the mark removed. We had a long talk about it. I asked her if she wanted to remove it. She said, "No, I like it." I said, "Terrific. Don't go changing yourself to please others. Soon people will know you because of your beauty mark . . ." The rest is history—Cindy is now an internationally successful model.

Are you getting the point? Everyone has an opinion. How can we as fallible human beings possibly decide the destiny of someone else? We can't. How can modeling schools possibly determine whether a person will become a successful model or not . . .?

When I was a struggling newlywed at sixteen, I attempted to become a model because a few friends suggested it and I had no real job skills to draw on. I mustered up every little ounce of courage to arrange an interview with a department store in Merritt Island, Florida. I turned up in my best (and only) outfit and the interviewer asked me to walk for her. I did and she abruptly told me, "You'll never model, you're too tall!" I was crushed. There are three significant points to this story. One, I allowed her to tell me

Ashley Quirco is a successful international model who also happens to be totally deaf. At first, agents and clients believed that her deafness would make it impossible for her to work, but she proved them all completely wrong. In fact, her hearing impairment allows her to focus much more intently on her work. Ashley's experience proves that belief in yourself is a vital ingredient of success.

RON CONTARSEY

what I couldn't do, two, I assumed that she knew more than I, and three, I didn't try again. I obviously didn't believe in myself enough to keep trying. Whatever you do you must believe in yourself. Where there is a will, there is a way!

There are dozens of different markets out there. If a model is in Peduka, Kentucky, and an agent there tells her she doesn't fit into that market, she may well be advised to try another career. A good agent will encourage that person to pursue another market, *not* another career. It takes time and effort to place a model in another market, something that many agents and modeling schools are not prepared to give. This means they're only likely to know their own market and have a limited ability to recognize raw talent. That's why you must do your research before you spend any time or money. Whether you go to a modeling school or dive right into the business, if modeling is your career choice, follow your heart.

Cindy Crawford's current comp-card (below) *and her first comp-card* (right).

J. BRADY

Photo credit: J. Brady

CYNTHIA CRAWFORD

Height: 5'9"	Bust: 34B	Hair: Lt. Brown
Weight: 116	Waist: 22	Eyes: Brown
Dress: 5–6	Hips: 34	Shoe: 8½

TALENT MANAGEMENT CORPORATION
STEWART

elite
John Casablancas
111 East 22nd Street, New York, New York 10010 Tel: 529 9800 Telex: 428546 Book

STEVEN MEISEL

PETER LINDBERGH

BILL KING

STEVEN MEISEL/PETER LINDBERGH/BILL KING

139

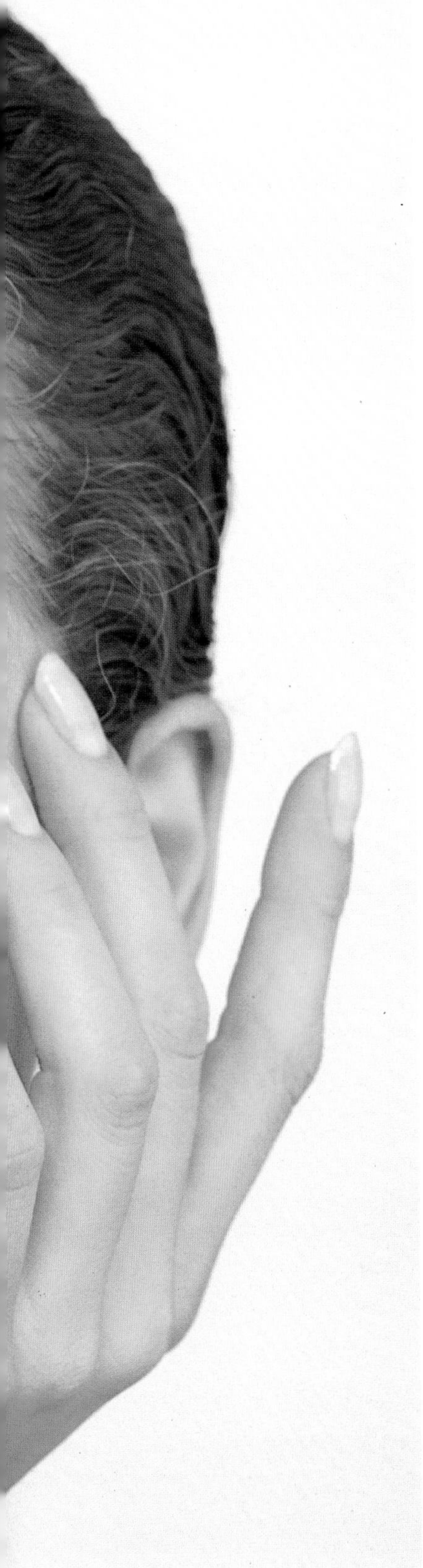

DAN ZAITZ

CHAPTER 8

NUTRITION AND EXERCISE

Facts about food

•

Eating disorders

•

Balancing your diet

•

Menu plans

•

Exercise

The secret of looking good depends as much on what you eat as what you wear. Good nutritional habits will help you cope with the stress and strain of a demanding job.

This chapter has been written by Curtis Brackenbury, president of Prime Corporation, a consulting company monitoring the principle of efficiency in physical fitness. True to his ideals, Curtis is enviably fit, having played eleven years of professional hockey, competed as a tri-athlete, completed the Iron Man competition in Hawaii, participated in the Americas Cup on Canada's 12-meter yacht, and interned at the Institute of Sports in Australia. He is married to an international fashion model and currently lectures and designs fitness programs for Elite models. With his wide experience in the health and fitness fields, and his inside knowledge of modeling, I knew that Curtis was the best person to write this chapter. A model is similar in many ways to a professional athlete—both make money with their bodies.

NUTRITION

Modeling is a career which is often influenced by the whims and wishes of other people, but nutrition and exercise are two areas over which you have complete control. What you eat will affect your personality, appearance, attitude and, most importantly, your performance. A balanced diet can give your skin a healthy glow, your hair that extra shine, your eyes that special brightness and your teeth that unforgettable gleam.

FACTS ABOUT FOOD

The nutrients in food supply energy, encourage growth and help keep the body working. Foods can be divided into three groups: carbohydrates, fats, and proteins. It is important to know what these are in order to balance your diet properly.

Carbohydrates

Carbohydrates are the body's favorite fuel, providing the energy for brain work and all physical activity. A balanced diet should include 50–60 percent carbohydrate and there are many delicious forms to choose from: corn, grains, potatoes, rice, beans, and fruit. These foods also contain roughage, more commonly known as fiber. A great plus is that fiber makes you chew more slowly and takes up more room in your stomach, so you actually eat less. To get the full benefit, you should drink water when eating foods containing lots of dry fiber. As with any food, if you eat more carbohydrate than you need, the excess will be stored in the body as fat.

Refined sugars are also carbohydrates, but they contain no valuable nutrients—they are an "empty" food. If you fill up on sugars (a Mars bar instead of a meal, for example), your diet will be unbalanced. In addition, you will not have the energy needed for a full day's work. Make sure you read all the labels on food products, and remember that any words ending in "ose," such as glucose and fructose, are also sugars and no better for you than refined white sugar. The same applies to honey and syrups. Remember, all sweet things are bad for your teeth, so try to cut down your consumption. Always carry a toothbrush so you can clean your teeth every time you eat.

Fats

Fats play an important role in the body. Apart from being the largest store of potential energy, they also cushion the internal organs and help keep the body warm. The average male has about 15 percent body fat, while the average female has about 25 percent. Fats play a major part in your appearance: if you have insufficient fat in your diet, your skin will become dry and your hair limp and dull. To get energy your body will begin to use protein, which should be used specifically for building muscle and repairing damaged tissue. As a rough guide, fats should account for 30 percent of your daily diet. If you're worried about cholesterol and heart disease, just make sure you opt for skimmed dairy products and polyunsaturated fats and oils.

Proteins

Protein is present in every cell in the human body—in fact, it is vital for growth and development of all tissues. It is found in such foods as meat, fish, poultry, nuts, peas, and beans. Protein should make up 10–15 percent of your daily diet. There is no advantage to be gained from eating more than the recommended amount as any excess is simply stored as fat and/or expelled in the urine.

Other nutrients
Vitamins

Although they are not a source of energy, vitamins are essential for health and normal body development. They cannot be made by the body, but are produced in plants and in animals which eat plants. If you eat a balanced diet, you will be getting all the vitamins you require; supplements should only be necessary for specific conditions on the recommendation of your doctor or dietitian. To preserve the vitamin content of fruit and vegetables, eat them raw or lightly cooked.

Iron
Iron is carried in the blood and is vital to well-being. A deficiency of iron can cause weakness, loss of appetite, reduce resistance to infection and, most importantly, lead to fatigue. This tends to be more common among women than men, mainly because of blood loss during menstruation. Female models should pay particular attention to iron intake when exercising during menstruation and if following a vegetarian diet. (In these situations an iron supplement may be necessary.) Some good sources of iron are lean red meat, liver, prunes, kidney beans, leafy green vegetables, and wholegrain bread.

Calcium
For many women, especially thin women, calcium deficiency can be a real problem. Calcium absorption tends to fall with age so the body draws on calcium deposits in the bones. This can lead to bones becoming thin and brittle—a condition called osteoporosis. To avoid this, make sure you get an adequate daily allowance of calcium by consuming dairy products, canned salmon and dark, leafy vegetables.

Water
The body needs about 2 pints of liquid a day. Of course, you'll need more when working or exercising in hot weather, perhaps even five or six times more than normal. But water is one thing you can happily consume in quantity with no ill effects. It's great for cleansing the system and keeping the skin clear, and doesn't have any calories. And another thing—foods which have a high water content, such as melons, cucumbers and celery, are also low in calories.

EATING DISORDERS

Modeling is a business that calls for lean good looks in both men and women, and it's all too easy to let preoccupations with weight dominate your life. If you're not one of the lucky ones who doesn't have to monitor every mouthful, you must devise a sensible nutrition and exercise program and avoid any unhealthy fads.

Unfortunately, some models develop a compulsion to be thin, going to extreme lengths to achieve their goals. This may involve periods of starvation (anorexia), or periods of heavy eating (bulimia), followed by purging with laxatives or self-induced vomiting. Apart from the damaging effects that anorexia and bulimia have on the body, such regimes do nothing for your looks and could eventually jeopardize your career.

Eating disorders are not simple conditions; they can lead to serious health problems and even death. Don't be afraid or embarrassed to admit to your problem. Talk to a professional who can help you to sort things out.

BALANCING YOUR DIET

The body needs many different nutrients to remain healthy, so it is essential to eat a variety of foods every day. One of the easiest ways of ensuring a balanced intake is to eat at least the minimum recommended daily servings from the following five food groups. The servings may be varied, depending on your age, sex and level of activity. No two people will have exactly the same needs, but everyone should have the minimum daily requirement.

Food groups	Suggested daily servings
Group 1 Breads, cereals, rice, pasta, wholegrain products	6–11 per day
Group 2 Fruit—apples, oranges, melons, berries, grapes, etc.	2–4 per day
Group 3 Vegetables – dark green leafy, deep yellow, dried beans and peas (legumes)	3–5 per day
Group 4 Meat, poultry, fish, eggs, beans, seeds, nuts	2–3 per day
Group 5 Dairy—milk, cheese, yogurt	2–3 per day (men) 3–4 per day (women) 4 per day (teenagers)

MENU PLANS

The following menu plans are based on the food groups above. The first has been devised for meat-eaters, the second for vegetarians. Both offer a minimum intake of 1500 calories. The right-hand column has additional and/or alternative items which may be included to bring the daily intake up to 2000 calories.

MEAT-EATERS' MENU	
1500 calories	Additions/ alternatives for 2000 calories
Breakfast ⅔ cup/2 oz bran cereal ½ 9-in banana 1 slice rye toast 1 cup/8 fl oz low- or non-fat milk	
Lunch 1 cup/8 fl oz split pea soup 1 slice wholewheat bread 2 oz roast chicken (skinned) 1 tsp mayonnaise 2 lettuce leaves 2 slices tomato 1 apple 1 cup/8 fl oz low- or non-fat milk	3 small crackers
Supper 3 oz lean steak, broiled 1 wholewheat roll 2 oz steamed broccoli 1 oz Mozzarella cheese 1 small boiled potato	2 small boiled potatoes 1 tsp margarine ⅓ 5-inch canteloupe
1 cup tea with lemon	
Snacks ¾ fresh pineapple	1 cup/8 oz non-fat yogurt 1¼ cups/4 oz fresh strawberries

PETER CHADWICK

PETER CHADWICK

VEGETARIAN MENU

1500 calories	Additions/ alternatives for 2000 calories
Breakfast ⅔ cup/2 oz bran cereal ½ 9-inch banana 1 slice raisin bread 1 tsp margarine 1 cup/8 fl oz low- or non-fat milk	 2 slices wholewheat toast 2 tsp margarine
Lunch 1½ cups/3 oz wholewheat pasta 1 cup/6 fl oz fresh tomato sauce 2 tsp Parmesan cheese 5 grapes mineral water	 1 cup/3 oz salad 2 tsp oil and vinegar dressing 15 grapes coffee, tea or water 3 small crackers
Supper 1 cup/8 fl oz split pea soup 1 cup/3 oz spinach salad topped with 1 medium sliced orange 2 tsp low-calorie dressing 1 small pumpernickel roll 1 cup/8 fl oz low- or non-fat milk 3 gingersnaps	 2 wholewheat rolls 1 fresh peach
Snacks 1 cup/8 oz non-fat yogurt ¾ cup/4 oz blueberries	 1 medium apple chopped into yogurt 2 tsp raisins

EXERCISE

Modeling is a business that demands elite physical characteristics. Your body is your livelihood, a fact you must always keep in mind. Success comes about through a combination of factors, but the most important is preparation. Perhaps you will be an overnight sensation, or maybe you will have to slog every step of the way. Whatever the case, preparation will lay the foundation for the future. It will enable you to stay healthy and maintain a steady income for a long period of time.

Wherever you go, no matter what continent, everyone talks about health and fitness. In Milan, Paris, New York, London and Tokyo the philosophy is the same: eat right, work out, look great. But first of all you must ask yourself some questions. What is right for me? What is right for my career?

PREPARING AN EXERCISE PLAN

Preparation involves taking a long, hard look at yourself, noting and highlighting your strengths, identifying and improving your weaknesses. In order to make this assessment, you need to consider the following things.

Fundamental qualities of a model

Whatever market you specialize in, good posture is a vital attribute in modeling. It must be combined with fluid body movements and good balance, both of which can be achieved by sensible exercise programs.

Workload

A model must know when particular markets are busiest so he or she can balance work and exercise demands efficiently. During intense periods of modeling your priority is work—exercise plays a lesser role. When work is quieter, exercise comes to the fore, giving you the opportunity to prepare your body for specific markets.

Time

Using your time efficiently and realistically is important. You must establish a schedule which allows you to complete your normal daily activities without overstretching yourself. You will be demoralized if you constantly set goals that you fail to meet.

Client demand and response

Feedback from the people you work for is extremely valuable. It can give you an insight to your market, help you identify what the client likes and dislikes, and thus help you be better prepared.

When you have examined each of these things and know what your time and temperament will allow you to do, you must take a long hard look at your body. Keeping your body in shape and in demand requires attention to three main things.

1 Posture

It is a common complaint among clients and photographers that too many models have poor posture: round shoulders, sway backs and small bulging stomachs. Designers and clients want models who will enhance their products, so you must practice holding yourself properly to eradicate these defects. Look at the photo below to see an example of good posture.

2 Balance

Professional models make it look easy, but spinning and twirling in front of cameras and bright lights, perhaps while wearing high heels or climbing stairs, is quite a skill. They mustn't "cheat" by using their arms for balance or looking at the ground—they must move instinctively and learn to "feel" where they are at all times. It requires constant practice to achieve good balance—to move naturally and easily without apparent regard for the surroundings. One step on the way to achieving this is to acquire

JOHN BECKETT

Good posture

Experienced models move with grace and agility, even under the most demanding conditions. Walking, dancing and twirling along the catwalk in front of a large and critical audience is not easy, but you can make it look easy when you have good muscle control.

ROLAND KING

muscular strength so you have greater control over your movements.

3 Muscle strength

Modeling often calls for movements to be repeated or for poses to be held for long periods. Apart from stamina, you will need good muscle control to make the movements graceful and smooth. Make a mental note of the sort of poses required in a standard modeling session and practice them at home. Stand in front of a full-length mirror, lift your arms, then let them drop to your side. Now exert some real muscle control by lifting them again slowly and pausing half way up for five seconds. Bring them back down slowly. Repeat this exercise with your legs and head. Concentrate on improving the movements that you find awkward or jerky. Remember, you may have to hold or repeat certain movements all day in a modeling session, so you must build up the muscle strength to perform as well at the end of a shoot as you did at the beginning.

In order to increase your strength, improve your posture and develop fluid movement patterns you must follow an exercise program. First of all you must work on body stability which is controlled by the "core." As you can see from the illustration, the core is a large area controlling the arms, legs, and neck. The muscles in the shaded areas control posture. It is most important to move the core muscles in a slow, controlled fashion.

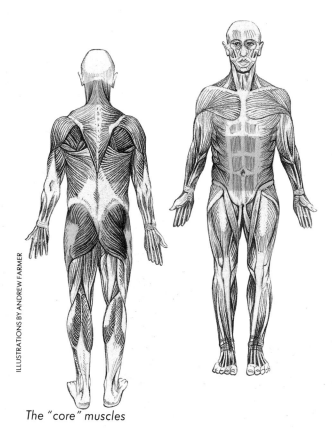

ILLUSTRATIONS BY ANDREW FARMER

150   The "core" muscles

Outlined below is a sequence of exercises which will help you to build up your muscles. For all the exercises, the following points *always* apply:

- Do all exercises slowly.

- Do all exercises in the full range of motion (i.e. extending yourself as far as you feel comfortable).

- Do each exercise in three stages:
  1 Lift up for a 4-second count
  2 Pause for 4 seconds
  3 Lower for a 4-second count.

- Stop at once if something hurts.

- Do not hold your breath.

- Count *out loud* while exercising—it will help you to breathe naturally.

- Each time you do an exercise, it is called a "repetition." Slowly build up your strength until you can complete 10 repetitions.

- 10 repetitions are called a "set." Your eventual goal is to complete 3–5 sets.

- Each side of the body is exercised separately. When you have completed one set of each exercise, change positions and work on the other side of the body.

- Remember that "form" is most important. Do not try to increase your range of action by moving other body parts. If your muscles cannot manage something, don't do it. As your strength increases, so will your range of flexibility.

In the first week or so of your exercise program, the aim is to make your body "aware." Try to do approximately 3 sets of exercises with 5 repetitions per set. Then progress to 3–5 sets of 10 repetitions per week.

CORE EXERCISES

Starting position for neck bends

1 Kneel on the floor, placing the hands on the floor 15 inches in front of the knees.
2 Keep the abdominal muscles tight and the pelvis tucked towards the back.
3 Keep the back straight and the eyes fixed on the ground.
4 Tuck the chin into the chest.

Backward neck bends

1 Adopt the starting position.
2 Slowly, on a 4-second count, keeping the shoulders steady, roll the head back.

3 Pause for 4 seconds.

4 Return to the starting position on a 4-second count. (Don't forget to count out loud).

Forward neck bends

1 Adopt the starting position.

2 Slowly, on a 4-second count, keeping the shoulders steady, roll the head forward.

3 Pause for 4 seconds at the end of your range of motion.

4 Return to the starting position on a 4-second count.

Side neck bends

1 Adopt the starting position.

2 Slowly, on a 4-second count, move your head to one side and try to touch your shoulder with your ear. Do not change your form.

3 Pause for 4 seconds at the terminal point.

4 Return to the starting position on a 4-second count.

5 Repeat the exercise on the other side.

Neck turns

1 Adopt the starting position.

2 Slowly, on a 4-second count, turn the head 90 degrees to the left.

3 Pause for 4 seconds.

4 Return to the starting position on a 4-second count.

5 Slowly, on a 4-second count, turn the head 90 degrees to the right.

6 Pause for 4 seconds.

7 Return to the starting position on a 4-second count.

Body side bends

1 Lie on your right side on the floor.

2 Secure your feet.

3 Tuck in your chin, keep your shoulders back, hold in your abdominal muscles and keep your buttocks tight.

4 Place your right arm across your chest.

5 Keep your left arm resting on the side of your body.

6 On a count of 4, lift the upper body and slide the left arm toward your knee.

7 Pause for 4 seconds in a position within your range of motion that allows you to keep your form and control. As your strength increases, you will be able to get closer to your knee.

8 Return to the starting position, on a count of 4.

9 Repeat the exercise on the other side.

Remember not to go past the point of control in any exercise.

Sit-ups

These exercises are designed to create strong abdominal muscles which hold in the stomach and strengthen the lower back, helping to prevent lower back pain. They are graded from 1–3 in order of difficulty, so you should start with the easiest and work your way up. As you "curl up" the upper back and shoulders, remember to push the abdominal muscles toward the floor. Do not secure your feet. On the return portion of the exercise, imagine the backbone being lowered inch by inch so you have complete control.

Starting position for sit-ups

1 Lie flat on the floor.

2 Bend the knees approximately 90 degrees.

3 Tuck in the chin.

4 Tilt the pelvis towards the chest.

5 Push the abdominal muscles toward the floor.

Level 1 sit-ups

1 Adopt the starting position.

2 Place your hands on your thighs.

3 Roll your head toward your chest.

4 Roll your shoulders forward, sliding your hands gently toward your knees.

5 On a count of 4, curl the upper body to the point where the lower back is just about to rise.

JOHN BECKETT

Body side bends

6 Hold this position for 4 seconds.
7 On a count of 4, return slowly to the starting position, lowering the vertebrae one by one.

Level 2 sit-ups
1 Adopt the starting position.
2 Place your hands across your chest.
3 Roll your head and shoulders forward.
4 Repeat steps 5–7 of level 1.

Level 3 sit-ups
1 Adopt the starting position.
2 Place your hands behind your head.
3 Roll your head and shoulders forward.
4 Repeat steps 5–7 of level 1.

This concludes the core exercises. Now it is time to use that stabilizing strength and develop balance and fluid body movement. The following exercises will give you a feeling of motion and control.

BEAM EXERCISES

The beam is a great and inexpensive way to enhance your modeling career. Get a length of 4 x 4-inch wood which is at least 6 feet long. (You may find it easier to get wood which is 2 inches thick; if so, buy two lengths and nail them together.) Before you start work on the beam, sandpaper the wood so there is no danger of splinters. Place the beam on the floor and you're ready to start.

The form

It is essential to adopt the correct posture for beam exercises: keep the back of the neck long and the chin drawn in; "pinch" the shoulder blades together, then lower them gently to keep shoulders back; pull the chest down and in by using the upper abdominals. Tighten the lower abdominals as if you want them to touch your back. Finally, clench the muscles in your buttocks. It will help if you can practice in front of a mirror, then you can see what the correct form looks like. As you become more familiar with the exercises, your body will feel more comfortable.

The first step

The toes are the first part to touch the beam; they should be used in a sensitive, gripping fashion. The heel is next; it should be lowered gently. To check your leg position look down: the knee should be in a straight line with the inside of the toe. The other foot is placed comfortably behind the heel of the foot in front. You may feel the foot moving in and out, trying to balance. This shakiness will decrease as the strength in your stabilizer muscles increases. Now, looking straight ahead, take a step forward as follows. Push the pelvis forward, shifting the weight on to the balls of your feet. Then swing the back leg forward and start the process again. Keep looking straight ahead at all times. Your hands and arms should be at your sides in a controlled but relaxed manner.

Learning to balance

It is important not to watch your feet or to worry about what is happening down below. The aim is to "feel and sense" what is happening. If you find it difficult to balance, turn your thumbs outwards as far as they can go. If you feel yourself swaying

1   2   3

to one side, don't flap your arms around to gain your balance. Try to correct your position by using the "core" muscles. For example, if you are swaying to the right, tighten up the muscles on the left side of the core. While all this is going on, don't forget your posture. It's important to maintain the correct "form" at all times.

Moving on the beam

Whether moving backwards or forwards on the beam, steps should always be taken in the same way: lead with the pelvis, feel with the toes, then lower the heel. When you get to the end of the beam, stop. Lift both heels, then pivot 180 degrees and face the other way. If the right leg is ahead, turn to your left; if the left leg is ahead, turn to your right. If you want to move sideways, the weight has to be transferred to the balls of the feet because the beam is narrow. Always maintain your form. If you lose control, stop, collect yourself and start again.

Tackle the following exercises in the sequence given. By working through them slowly and methodically you will acquire the muscle strength to achieve good balance and control. You might like to start by practicing them on the floor. Once you feel comfortable, move to the beam.

Level 1 beam
1 Adopt the correct form.
2 Step on to the beam, looking straight ahead.
3 Walk slowly to the end of the beam.
4 Stop, then return backwards along the beam.

Level 2 beam
1 Adopt the correct form.

2 Step on to the beam looking straight ahead.
3 Lift up on your toes one foot at a time, then both feet together.
4 Make slow, controlled swing turns, first to the left, then to the right.
5 Gradually build up speed.
6 Hop on one foot, then the other.
7 Stand sideways on the beam.
8 Slide feet sideways along the beam.

Level 3 beam
1 Adopt the correct form.
2 Stand sideways on the beam.
3 Cross the right leg over the left.
4 Bend and touch the beam with the left hand.
5 Repeat, crossing the left leg over the right.
6 Bend and touch the beam with the right hand.
7 Lift one leg and hold for 5 seconds.
8 Lift one leg and lower the body as far as you can without losing your form.
9 Hold for 5 seconds, counting out loud.
10 Repeat with the other leg.

Advanced beam work
- Try doing all the previous exercises with your eyes closed. Really try to feel and sense where you are at all times.

- Ask somebody to throw you a ball. Try to catch it without moving your head and losing your form. Follow the ball with your eyes. This ability will stand you in good stead for fashion shows and camera work.

Now you are ready to start doing some serious training on the beam. The following movements are designed specifically for models.

1 The correct "form" on the beam.
2 Walking along the beam.
3 Moving sideways along the beam.
4 Lifting one leg on the beam.
5 Catching a ball without losing balance or form.

4 5

Half turn

1 Stand on the beam with the right foot forward. Most of your weight should be on the back foot.
2 Step forward, transferring the weight on to the ball of the right foot.
3 Twist your upper body to the desired direction and pivot on the ball of the right foot.
4 As you near completion of the turn, gently place the toes of the left foot on the beam.
5 Transfer your weight to the left foot while the right foot is prepared either in a stance position or is ready to walk out of the turn.

Hip movement

1 Walk along the beam keeping the upper core and shoulders steady while moving the hips.
2 Then walk along the beam keeping the hips steady while practicing shoulder movements. Remember, the runway walk requires the shoulders to be tilted slightly back.
3 Once you get control, practice moving the hips and shoulders at the same time.

Walking

Practice walking along the beam on the balls of your feet. This will help you to move well when wearing high heels.

Standing

Photographic work requires two kinds of strength: one allows you to stand motionless for long periods of time, the other allows you to move gracefully. Sometimes you may even be required to hold bizarre positions, such as standing on one leg with arms stretched out. Have a look at current fashion magazines and see how the models are posing. Then practice on the beam in front of a mirror until you are strong and graceful.

1 Stand on your right foot.
2 Bend the knee and hold the left foot 2 inches off the beam in front of the body to a count of 4.
3 Gradually raise the foot until it is 12 inches off the beam to a count of 4.
4 Finally, raise the foot until it is 24 inches off the beam to a count of 4.

Once you can do 3 sets of 10 repetitions, increase the holding time progressively to 30 seconds, then to 1 minute.

Conclusion

This exercise program was designed specifically for models by looking at the requirements of the profession and the demands on the body. Used properly, it will give you a better understanding of your body and your job. Modeling is a business of dollars and sense. Look after your body with a balanced diet and sensible exercise, and you'll reap dividends in terms of health, appearance and career.

I am particularly grateful to Dr Philip Factor for his valuable assistance, and to Robert Gajda, co-author of *Total Body Fitness*, whose foundation philosophy is the basis of this exercise program. (The books I found especially helpful in writing this chapter are listed in a bibliography on page 170.)

Opposite Energetic dancing can be a good alternative way of keeping supple.
Below left Half turn.
Below right Walking on the balls of the feet.

CHAPTER 9

HANDLING YOUR FINANCES

Agents' fees
•
Choosing an accountant
•
Keeping records
•
Tax deductions
•
Foreign taxes

MICHAEL ROBERTS

It's important to set aside time in order to organize your finances. Sifting through your receipts and invoices on a regular basis will help prevent a once-yearly filing nightmare.

Every time I overheard a model discussing her finances, the same accountant's name was always mentioned—Debra Lessin. Personal recommendation is the best reference anyone can have, so I knew my search for a good accountant was over.

Debra is president and owner of D.J. Lessin & Associates Inc., Certified Public Accountants. The firm provides a wide range of accounting and tax services with primary emphasis on tax planning and compliance for professional, creative and entrepreneurial small businesses and individuals. Debra began her firm in 1984 after eight years of experience in both "Big 8" public accounting and the corporate sector. She combines her business savvy and technical expertise with a flair for creativity and humor that, for her, makes people the most important aspect of being a CPA—not just the numbers. Taking all these things into account, it became obvious that Debra was the ideal person to write this chapter. (Note that, for simplicity, the accountant is referred to as "she" throughout.)

Remember that each country has its own tax rules and regulations which tend to change from year to year. Debra has written only about American tax laws, as those are the ones which probably apply to you most. The paragraph about the new witholding tax being applied to foreign models in the UK has been written by Vinod Vadgama (ACCA, ATTI) of Leigh Carr, Chartered Accountants, in London, experts in British accounting procedures.

Being a model requires a lot more than a pretty face. It is extremely important to organize yourself sensibly *and* be responsible for your money. This chapter offers you general guidance about handling your finances, but it is in no way sufficient to replace a personal accountant. Please do not take this area lightly. Many models who have not paid their taxes have ended up in very serious trouble. Whenever you make or spend money, it must be accounted for.

AGENTS' FEES

While you may think that you work for your agent, the reality is that your agent works for you. Webster's dictionary defines an agent as "one who acts for or in the place of another by authority from him." Your agents acts for you in promoting you and arranging bookings on your behalf.

An agent's resources, experience and staff all have a price tag. You pay your agent a commission on the monies you earn through their professional efforts. Commission percentages vary from agency to agency and from city to city. The industry norm is 15 or 20 percent. One of the services your agent provides is to bill clients for your bookings and to collect on that billing. Upon settlement, your agency will send you a check for the booking fee minus their commission.

Your check may also reflect deductions for any business expenses you have incurred if you have asked your agency to pay them on your behalf. These expenses may also include some general promotional costs, such as headsheet expenses, which are arranged by the agency on behalf of you and the other models they represent. Organizing payment of such expenses is an administrative burden for the agency, as well as a cash flow drain. Business expenses are really your responsibility—unless, of course, the client agrees to cover them as part of the booking agreement.

Deductions for cash advances and the agency's commission will generally be the *only* deductions from your check. Taxes will *not* be deducted because you are not considered to be an employee of your agency. You are, in fact, self-employed. Your agent merely facilitates your billing, collection and promotional activities.

Being self-employed means that *you* are solely responsible for paying any taxes owing to state/provincial and federal authorities. This responsibility is often overlooked, particularly by models new to the business. It is both short-sighted and foolish to focus on only the glamorous aspects of the industry. It is important to remember that, as a model, you are also a self-employed *business* person. Your business is modeling. While you may not find the "numbers" aspect of the business particularly interesting, you should never mock or underestimate its importance.

As soon as you begin your modeling career, find yourself a Certified Public Accountant (CPA), or a Chartered Accountant (CA) in Canada. Financial horror stories abound and circulate throughout the business about models who neglect the financial aspects of their careers through fear, ignorance, laziness, or a combination of all three. The stories always have the same conclusion: the models incur heavy penalties for late payment of tax, non-payment of estimated tax and late filings of tax returns. There is also compound interest due on the tax owed. You can avoid such penalties and the horrible hole they leave in your pocket if you hire a good CPA from the outset.

CHOOSING AN ACCOUNTANT

It is important to find an accountant with the CPA designation because there are many accountants and tax preparers in business today who do not keep up with the constantly changing tax laws. An accountant who has earned the educational and professional credentials to obtain the CPA designation *must* keep abreast of tax laws in order to maintain a license.

However, finding someone who simply knows the tax laws is not enough—your accountant should also be familiar with the modeling business. Unless the nature of the industry is understood, you can be sure that certain deductions or items pertinent to your taxes will be overlooked.

While you must take overall responsibility for record-keeping and documentation, your accountant should guide you about what is and is not important. She should spend time discussing your career with you and finding out how you keep track of your income and expenses. She should then help design a simple and functional record-keeping system for you that can be easily used on a regular basis. Nothing complicated is required. However, you must accept that you will have to do *some* paperwork if you want to be a successful model. Without this you cannot prove that you have spent money for business related expenses. The end result: you pay more in taxes. Perish the thought!

Technical expertise aside, perhaps the most important facet of the relationship with your accountant is trust. Are you comfortable with your accountant as a person? Does she make herself available to answer your questions or take your calls? Does she communicate with clients on a regular basis in an understandable manner, be it by phone, letter, or in person? Apart from keeping abreast of tax laws, does your accountant also provide you with tax-planning options and

opportunities? Does she tell you in simple terms what you need to know and do? Does she have the resources and business network to direct you to people who can help you invest your money when that day comes?

Too often people fear their accountants. In the long run, that fear will result in an unsatisfying relationship. Whatever preconceived ideas you have about accountants, it *is* possible to find some who care about people and who communicate with their clients in English, not "accountantese!" You want an accountant who enjoys working with people in a one-to-one professional relationship and who believes her function is to save the clients' money. The numbers become secondary; it's the people who matter. How do you find such a person? Ask your fellow models for recommendations. The best testimonial an accountant can ever have is a satisfied client.

KEEPING RECORDS

Now you've realized that a model must be financially responsible, you need to learn just what that responsibility entails. While your accountant can and will apply the tax laws to the annual financial result of your modeling career, you need to provide the requisite detail and appropriate information. This chapter focuses only on the information relevant to your business.

Many young people are attracted to the modeling industry because it offers the possibility of financial success and independence. While it is perfectly possible to achieve both these things, you should be aware that when you start your career your outgoing cash may well exceed your income. Among the out-of-pocket expenses you will incur are prints and composites, cosmetics, taxis, air fares, hotels, and so forth. You need to keep track of each and every expense in an organized manner on a consistent basis.

Sometimes it can be hard to distinguish between a personal and business expense, particularly when your physical self is so much a part of your business. However, once you learn the fine distinctions, be sure to keep track of all relevant expenses. In fact, it's advisable to keep track of everything you spend your money on, just in case you need to itemize it later. Your accountant can evaluate the significance of each expense in relation to your business. If you don't keep track of your expenses, you will pay taxes on your gross income paid to you through your agency. This does not benefit you financially because that overpaid tax money belongs in your pocket, helping you to build a secure financial future.

A simple way to keep track of expenses is by using the "envelope method." Start off by buying eighteen 9 x 13 in envelopes and a file box to keep them in. Next, in the upper left-hand corner of

ILLUSTRATIONS BY ANDREW FARMER

each envelope, write the year and expense category. Categories applicable to your business include the following:

- Accounting fees
- Auto expenses
- Business meals and entertainment
- Business gifts
- Commissions
- Dues and publications (union fees, fashion magazines, etc.)
- Educational seminars (acting classes)
- Office supplies
- Postage
- Prints and composites
- Professional grooming expenses
- Supplies (wardrobe and cosmetics)
- Taxis and other local transportation
- Telephone
- Travel: out of town transportation
  out of town meals
  out of town lodging
  out of town cabs, buses, car rental

Now that you have your envelopes and an idea of the specific categories, you can begin to use them. Whenever you incur a particular expense, place the receipt in the appropriate envelope. If you don't obtain a receipt for some reason, you need to keep a written note of the expense. For example, you may tend to forget small, out-of-pocket expenses such as taxis, but over a period of time, these expenses add up. At the end of every day in every week, sort out your receipts and place them in the appropriate envelope.

If you keep up your records on a regular basis, it will become a habit and save you the

cumbersome task of organizing your receipts at the end of the year. Leaving such tasks to the last minute will sap your energy, fray your temper and be an insurmountable task for your memory. Documentation is undoubtedly the key to lowering your tax liability and is a valuable safeguard against the day when the Internal Revenue Service/Revenue Canada might choose to audit your tax return. While an audit is always an unnerving experience, your mind (and your accountant's) will be calmed if your records are organized and well documented.

Occasionally, you may need to add some more specific information on the face of a receipt to indicate its relevance to your business. Examples relating to specific expenses are described below—some relate to information required by law for tax reporting purposes, others relate to certain expenses specific to the modeling industry.

TAX DEDUCTIONS

Travel

Sometimes modeling work may necessitate traveling to other cities for a client booking, or simply to experience another market. Career advancement may even require relocating to another city for a period of time. Expenses incurred in traveling "away from home" are business deductions if it can be established that the expenses were incurred as part of your business. This "away from home" test is not met unless your work requires you to be away from the general area of your "tax home" for a period substantially longer than an ordinary day's work, including a time allowance for sleep or rest. (In Canada your deductions for day trips are permitted at the discretion of the tax department.)

Your "home" for tax purposes is considered to be:

1 Your regular or principal place of business, **or**

2 Your regular place of abode in a real and substantial sense, if you have no regular principal place of business because of the nature of your work.

Where you have multiple areas of business activity or places of regular employment, the principal place is treated as your tax home for purposes of determining your travel expenses deduction. In determining your principal place of business, you should consider:

1 The time spent on business activity in each area
2 The amount of business activity in each area
3 The amount of the resulting financial return in each area

The length and nature of your stay away from your principal place of business is of prime importance in determining when you are "away from home." If your presence is temporary, you are "away from home." If your presence is for an indefinite period of time, your new location will become your new "tax home" and you may not deduct travel expenses while there. If employment is anticipated to last for one year and does, in fact, last for one year but less than two years, the IRS presumes that the employment is not temporary. An expected or actual stay of two years or longer will be considered an indefinite stay, regardless of any other facts or circumstances. If, however, you are a Canadian citizen and maintain your residential status and file a Canadian income tax return, you may continue to deduct your travel expenses.

If you work consistently in one city, it is relatively easy to determine where your tax home is and when you are "away from home." But as your career progresses, and you find your time divided between different cities, you may find it harder to define your "home."

The point of determining your "home" is to calculate what expenses incurred by you in traveling away from home are deductible. Once you know what these are, keep track of them.

The following expenses are ordinarily deductible while traveling away from home:

- Travel, meals and lodging
- Telephone
- Reasonable expenditures for laundry and cleaning
- Transportation between your place of lodging and place of business

A deduction for the cost of meals and lodging while away from home is limited to amounts which are not lavish or extravagant. You may deduct a documented amount for the actual amount of meal expenses while away from home, or you may elect to claim deductions for meal expenses as follows:

$14 per day for travel that requires a stay of less than 30 days in one general locality

and/or

$9 per day for travel that requires a stay of 30 days or more in one such general locality.

Note These *per diems* are subject to change, but in Canada they do not apply.

You may claim this "standard meal allowance" as long as you can substantiate the time, place and business purpose of the travel. While opting for this may save you time in obtaining, organizing and documenting your receipts, it will probably result in a lower deduction than actual expenses incurred. The choice is yours. Remember to keep your calendar of business activities up to date. You may need to reconstruct your business days away from home in order to claim this standard meal allowance.

For expenses incurred in tax years beginning after January 1st, 1987, it is vital to segregate your expenses for business meals incurred while away from home from your other travel expenses. Tax deductions for meals are now limited to 80 percent of the amount incurred. The 80 percent limit applies to any expense for food or beverage, including taxes and tips. Transportation expenses to and from the meal are not subject to the 80 percent limit.

Expenses for entertainment that directly precedes or follows a *bona fide* and substantial business discussion are deductible, even though incurred as good will. The business discussion, however, must be the principal reason for the combined entertainment and business.

Focus for a moment on your modeling business. You are constantly meeting with your agents, bookers, photographers and stylists. These meetings may result in business meals and entertainment expenses. In order to secure a deduction for tax purposes, you must provide substantiation and documentation. Always obtain an original receipt. While your cancelled check may provide proof of payment, it is not in itself, appropriate documentation.

Always remember to note on the face of each receipt the five Ws: Who, What, When, Where and Why. The receipt itself should indicate where and when, but you need to document who you were with, what their business relationship to you was, and why you were meeting. If you think about it, a large part of a model's life is business related.

Once you realize that and get into the habit of documenting your calendar and receipts with the necessary information, you will have valid business deductions, reduce your tax liability and, most importantly, be able to prove the validity of your business deductions.

Transportation and automobile expenses

Such things as travel by air, rail, bus, taxi and other forms of public transportation, as well as the cost of driving and maintaining an automobile, are deductible business expenses for models. However, commuting expenses to and from work are never deductible. As a model, your residence is generally your business locale, so strictly speaking, you don't ever really commute! Remember, the agency is not your office—it's your agent's.

Only the business part of auto expenses are deductible, so keep a daily log of your business mileage to and from jobs, auditions, interviews and meetings with your agents and photographers. This evidence is necessary to support your deduction. Also be sure to keep track of the purchase price of your auto or lease arrangement and your expenses for gasoline, oil, repairs, tires and accessories, insurance, wash and polish, licenses, interest, business parking and tolls.

Alternatively, you may be able to claim a standard mileage rate for business mileage. Parking fees and tolls are deductible in addition to the standard mileage rate. While this alternative method may diminish the need to keep detailed records of certain auto expenses, do keep in mind that for newer cars used in business, you will probably receive a lower deduction than a detailed accounting of actual expenses.

FOREIGN TRAVEL

Your career as a model may take you to foreign lands to explore new markets. There is a natural, though incorrect, assumption among models that as long as you are not in the US, you are not taxed on any income earned. As a US citizen, you are taxable on your worldwide earnings, so it is essential to keep track of your earnings and expenses whenever you travel abroad. In fact, it is very important to keep this information separate from your US expenses and sources of income.

Expenses for travel outside the US must be allocated between the business and personal parts of the trip. As long as you can prove that a personal vacation was not a major consideration in making the trip, no allocation will be necessary.

You may find that although European business trips open your eyes to new places and add to the status of your career, they may initially cost you more than you earn, particularly when you

consider meals and lodging. If this is the case, good bookkeeping may allow you to offset your foreign losses against your US source income and save you US taxes. Foreign withholding tax is based on your gross earnings and is usually covered by a tax treaty with the US. Read the information about foreign taxes on page 163, but call your accountant for more specific instructions before you travel.

Entertainment

The 80 percent limit applicable to business meals incurred while away from home overnight (see page 161), also applies to other business meals and entertainment. Business meals are only deductible under the following conditions:

1 The meal is "directly related to" or "associated with" the active conduct of a trade or business.
2 The expense is not lavish or extravagant under the circumstances.
3 You are present at the meal.

The business discussion requirement, however, does not apply where you eat alone away from home overnight in pursuit of your business. The 80 percent limit applies to any expense for food or beverages (including taxes and tips), and any item which relates to an activity which is generally considered to constitute entertainment, amusement, or recreation.

Generally, a deduction for entertainment expenses may not exceed the portion which is "directly related" to your business. There are three conditions for an entertainment expense to meet the "directly related" test:

1 You must have had more than a general expectation of deriving income, or some other specific business benefit, at some indefinite future time.
2 You must engage in active conduct of business with the person being entertained.
3 The active conduct of business must be the principal aspect of the combined business and entertainment.

Wardrobe

Contrary to common belief, a model's entire wardrobe is *not* a deductible business expense. You are only allowed to deduct those wardrobe items which you use *solely* for modeling. Clothing or shoes that you wear on weekends or at other non-working times are not deductible. It is advisable to note on the face of each receipt exactly why that particular item was required only for business (say, a specific shoot), and how it is not applicable to general use. Dry cleaning and tailoring related to your work and business wardrobe are also deductible.

Commissions

The commissions you pay your agency are deductible business expenses. At the end of each year, your agency will provide you with a Form 1099 (T5 slip in Canada) to report the monies paid to you in the calendar year. Before you determine your commission deduction, be sure to ask each agency how it reports the amount stated on Form 1099. Some agencies report "net," which means that the commission is already deducted from the amount reported. Other agencies report your "gross" non-employee earnings, which means that *you* must deduct the commission as a business expense from the gross amount reported. There is no consistency in the method of reporting among agencies or cities. You must always make it your business to know your agency's procedures and the applicable commission percentage. The Form 1099 you receive will also be the main source of accumulating your income for tax reporting purposes.

FOREIGN TAXES

This is a complicated area of tax law. Special rules may apply if you are out of the US for more than 365 days, or become a *bona fide* foreign resident. Your accountant will give you specific advice.

If you simply work abroad from time to time, make sure you keep track of all your business activities and that each agency you work for provides you with specific details of your earnings, including deductions for commissions, expenses and any taxes witheld. A witholding tax has recently been introduced in the UK as an anti-avoidance measure to prevent foreign models and others from avoiding tax both in the UK and their home countries. As of May 1st, 1987, the payer (the agency or the client) is obliged to deduct basic rate tax from any payment which arises in any way, directly or indirectly, from work performed in the UK. This means that on work performed outside the UK but paid for within, no tax needs to be witheld. This legislation also covers payment of expenses, such as airline tickets, on behalf of foreign models. In such cases the expenses paid are treated as net of tax and the payer has to account for taxes on them by "grossing up." Even if payment is made to a company or individual resident in the UK, tax must still be deducted. It may be possible to offset the tax witheld against your US tax liability or repayment in accordance with a double tax agreement with the US.

Witholding tax is also deducted from payment which arises from work performed in Canada.

Canadian models who work in the US may be subject to witholding taxes, depending on the length of their stay, the amount earned and the relevant treaty agreements. Once again, it is important to discuss this with your personal accountant.

When tax is witheld, you must always obtain a certificate showing the amount deducted. The UK Inland Revenue has a standard form called FEU 2. (In Canada the equivalent is known as an NR4 form.) You must keep it in a safe place as no duplicate can be issued by the person who has deducted the tax.

CONCLUSION

By now you must realize the importance of keeping good records. You must also be aware that you have sole responsibility for paying your taxes. While everyone focuses on April 15th (in Canada April 30th), the filing date for tax returns, as the critical deadline, there are other important tax dates that self-employed people should be aware of. The tax laws require you to pay in 90 percent (in Canada 100 percent) of your tax liability before April 15th (in Canada April 30th), either through estimated payments or withholding. Since you are self-employed, you will generally be required to make estimated payments on April 15th, June 15th, September 15th and January 15th of the following year. (In Canada the dates are March 31st, June 30th, September 30th, and December 31st.) You must not only consider any income taxes you may owe, but also self-employment taxes (social security/Canada Pension Plan) and state/provincial taxes. If you fail to make the appropriate estimated tax payments, you will be penalized. A variation on this rule is to pay estimated taxes based on your previous year's tax liability. Doing this in the early years of your career will protect you from penalties as your income increases.

All the information given here may seem rather overwhelming, but it can only benefit you in the long run. As your career progresses, financial planning may become even more vital. You may consider various retirement plan options available for self-employed individuals.

Modeling should be fun, but it should also provide you with tangible financial rewards. It is a business and you must always remember to treat it as such. This way you will be more aware of your financial responsibilities to the government and to yourself.

CHAPTER 10

COMMERCIAL ACTING

Getting a foot in the door

•

Commercial acting opportunities

•

Training

•

Glossy and résumé

Acting classes do far more than simply
teach you how to act. They also help you
to develop confidence and poise, two
vital attributes that will aid your career,
no matter what direction you finally
choose to pursue.

I decided to include commercial acting in this book because it offers such incredible opportunities to models. This chapter explains how to make the transition from fashion model to actor. Perhaps you can even think of some models who have made the transition successfully—Lauren Hutton, Farrah Fawcett, Cybill Shepherd.

In the following pages I outline the concept of commercial acting, make you aware of the (normally unmentioned) resistance you will meet from the acting community, and advise you on the organization of your glossy and résumé. There are books, classes and seminars which can give you detailed direction on how to pursue an acting career. This chapter merely aims to help you decide if an acting career holds any interest for you.

If you are currently a model and acting definitely interests you, be prepared! In the beginning, models-turned-actors are disliked by the acting profession, so they must work extremely hard to earn the professional actor's respect.

> 66 *Models should know that if they can really act, every door is opened to them.* 99
>
> Terry Berland
> Casting director

GETTING A FOOT IN THE DOOR

Commercial acting is one of the easiest areas for a model to get into, but few people in the acting world believe that modeling is a suitable background for anything other than modeling. Actors tend to think that models acquire acting jobs based upon their looks rather than talent or any special skills. Ask any seasoned actors how they feel about models becoming actors and you'll get some pretty strong reactions, often resentful and cynical. Many of these actors might have been struggling for years—moonlighting as waiters or waitresses, taking interminable classes and going on endless auditions—only to lose countless jobs to new, young whipper-snappers who may be more attractive. Naturally, they become disheartened.

Ask casting agents how much they expect to get from a model in a casting session, and they generally have high hopes. However, they are often let down by models who have not bothered to find out what a commercial casting or audition requires. Is it any wonder that models have a reputation for laziness and stupidity? This sloppy approach creates many hours of frustration and irritation; it is not the agents' responsibility to teach models how to audition, but they do have to fill the needs of their clients, so they endure the pain of casting with inexperienced models.

These harsh facts are intended to give you some insight so you will be better prepared to handle any discomfort that comes your way. If you wish to be accepted and respected you must play by the industry rules. Be sensitive and understanding of the acting community and the rough road ahead will be more tolerable for everyone.

COMMERCIAL ACTING OPPORTUNITIES

There are two types of commercials which frequently cast models.

"Photomatics" (sometimes called "anamatics") are photographs taken by a still photographer. They are converted to video using special techniques to give the feeling of movement, as in an ordinary film. This type of commercial is less expensive and faster to produce than a moving commercial. It also gives new actor/models a chance to see what it takes to produce a commercial and provides valuable experience to add to their acting résumés.

The second type of commercial involves real movement and may have speaking or non-speaking parts. Models cast for this type of commercial may find themselves doing anything — modeling clothing, advertising a store, selling a mattress, buying a car, opening a bank account—you name it!

Speaking parts usually require voice training. Frequently the client will request models who can speak as well as act, but very often they'll cast for the model's looks alone. If the model looks right but is inarticulate or has a regional accent, dubbing or looping will be necessary. For example, a Kentucky accent might alienate customers in New York, so the model will mouth the words during filming and an acceptable voice-over will be dubbed later. Be warned—having a regional accent will severely limit your speaking parts. Voice training will become necessary if you are serious about acting.

In both photomatics and ordinary commercials parts are available for principals and extras.

A principal part is the position held by the featured actor in a commercial. That actor is the representative of the product the consumer will focus on, and the part may be either a speaking or non-speaking role.

> 66 *Theater is basically the root of all the performing arts, especially acting. It can also help in commercials and in front of the still camera because you can perform for the still camera as you do for the moving camera.* 99
>
> John Crosby
> Agent/manager

Extra parts, which may be speaking or non-speaking, are held by people who are strategically placed to fill unwanted space in a commercial. Never underestimate the importance of these parts; an extra can always be upgraded. Being an extra is a terrific opportunity to learn the inside workings of commercial production without the stress of being a principal. It allows you to observe what is required of the principal actors, the creative process involved and the roles of the production team. Never reject a chance to learn something new—it could bring you that bit nearer to your goal.

> *Even though models may not come into the modeling world with the head and heart of an actor, they should at least learn commercial acting technique, so that they can handle a piece of copy, speak well on camera and audition. In knowledge there is power and confidence. You can expect no one to have confidence in you if you don't have confidence in yourself.*
>
> Michael Baird
> TV and film agent

TRAINING

Regardless of what country or market the commercials you wish to audition for are aimed at, *you must have proper training.* As I became more experienced as a print agent, I wanted to learn more about the commercial acting business, so I took an on-camera commercial acting class. It took eight weeks and was an incredible learning experience. It's amazing to learn things that the professionals make look so simple: how to handle a product so that the consumer can read it; timing the copy (dialogue) while handling the product; learning how to bite into a hamburger (there are specific classes available to teach people the art of eating on camera). You'll also learn techniques

> *I try to teach models how to fantasize and project their feelings in front of the camera— projecting is acting.*
>
> Di Vidos
> Modeling coach and manager

> *Training is the only way that they'll learn how to get their message across in one minute. They can practice in a workshop situation. It's different than posing in front of a still camera.*
>
> Terry Berland
> Casting director

> *Fashion agencies send headsheets to all casting directors and agents as those people are constantly looking for new faces. When they call us we are peppered with questions about specific models: Where are they from? Can they work in the US? Do they have regional accents? Do they have any training? Can they handle copy yet? It's imperative that they learn if they wish to compete on a professional level.*
>
> Michael Baird
> TV and film agent

for psyching yourself up for auditions and overcoming intimidating directors. The list could go on and on. The amount of training that *you* require will become obvious as you get involved in the business.

Randy Kirby is a successful model-turned-actor who regularly appears in commercials and even gives seminars about commercial acting all over the United States. He talked to me about his experiences and attitudes towards his work.

"Acting in TV commercials is an awful lot of fun. It can also be very demanding—doing take after take until it is exactly right. To me, it's an art form, just like photography. My advice to aspiring actors is, strive to be the very best you can, and always be looking for ways to improve."

While commercial acting can be a regular and lucrative source of income (particularly with repeat fees), you might begin to aspire to "higher things." If you develop serious theatrical ambitions, for example, you would be well advised to undertake proper theatrical training at a reputable drama school. It is rare to find a theatre professional who gives much credit for commercial acting experience. It just isn't in the same league.

> *At auditions, women should take a pair of flat shoes in case they have to read with a man who is shorter. They should also take plenty of ribbons, barrettes, rubber bands and a comb and brush as they may be able to tailor their look for a specific role. A good prop for men is a pair of horn-rim glasses. The bottom line is to find out as much as you can about the character you're auditioning for before you get there.*
>
> Randy Kirby
> Actor/model

John Rubano is an actor/comedian based in Chicago, who modeled briefly to keep the wolf from the door. He began his acting career by taking classes in improvisation. Following the advice of others, he signed on with five different agencies—something he later discovered was a complete waste of time as the agencies all get the same calls from the same casting people. His advice to aspiring actors is to sign on with one good agent who recognizes talent and takes the time to get to know the clients.

Since his professional acting debut about a year and a half ago, John has enjoyed growing success. He has performed comedy routines in clubs, made commercials, acted on stage and television, and appeared in movies. Describing his attitude to auditions, John has a refreshingly honest and candid approach. "I don't get nervous any more because I realize that it doesn't really matter if you screw up. There will always be another audition." His improvisation classes have obviously given him confidence and presence. "I don't like auditions for commercials. Cold copy that someone from an ad agency has written doesn't do anything for me. But I can put a lot of feeling into the comedy that I do and I can feel something for that."

What is John's advice to someone who wants to break into serious acting? In his words: "You have to believe in yourself. It's a dangerous business. You either make it, or you don't. There's very little in between."

Of course, your experiments with acting may not persuade you to take it up as a career. Perhaps you'll be more interested with the production end of it. There's no telling what the future holds for you!

> *If you give your dreams a shot and it doesn't work out, at least you tried. Nothing is worse than sitting around when you are fifty or sixty and saying, 'God dammit—I should have done it.' There's nothing worse than that.*
>
> John Rubano
> Actor/comedian

GLOSSY AND RÉSUMÉ

The acting world's equivalent of a portfolio is a good black and white head shot and a professionally laid out résumé. A fashion model's composite will not suffice for a commercial client. You must adhere to the acting industry requirements if you wish to be accepted and appreciated. Before you invest any money in your acting career you should first consult an acting agent. Most modeling agencies have film divisions or affiliated agencies that handle all their acting requirements. If you are fortunate enough to be a model with a print agency which has a film associate, your transition from modeling to acting will be easier.

A glossy is a black and white photograph measuring 8 x 10 in showing your head and part of your shoulders. Your first and last names are normally printed below the photo. Your eyes should be level with the camera. Avoid tilting your

STEPHEN WOLTER

JOHN RUBANO

> *Shoot your glossy with a photographer who normally shoots for actors. I want a regular head shot that really looks like the person and conveys their personality.*
>
> Jane Alderman
> Casting director

BETH BEHRENDS

MARC HAUSER

A model's comp-card (above) and glossy (right).

head or shrugging your shoulders. This type of body language can suggest indecision or insecurity. You are selling a product, so it is necessary to look like a sales person—decisive and confident! (You may see character actors who have silly photos; this does not apply to models.)

Your character, attitude, wardrobe, make-up and hairstyle should all be consistent with the image that you want to project. Avoid loud fabrics and distracting jewelry. Keep it clean and simple. Avoid any "fashion model" influence. Remember that you are appealing to the mass public, so maintain the "commercial" concept.

A résumé is a one-page, typewritten history of your related experience. It should be the same size as your glossy as it is stapled to the back of it, printed side out. It should have details of you and your agency, and clearly list your accomplishments over no more than the previous two or three years. A typical order of listing might read as follows: name, address, phone number, social security number (when appropriate in the country), height, weight, unions, agency,

appropriate education and training, theater, film and commercial experience, special skills (including foreign languages), talents, and finally, your special interests. Do not put any kind of modeling experience on your acting résumé. Résumés will vary from market to market and person to person. This outline is only for your general guidance. Your agent will assist you in the preparation of your résumé.

Every country has its own rules and regulations. Always ask about the commercial acting opportunities and requirements whenever you travel abroad. It's possible that the experience and training you have in one market may not be appreciated in another. For example, you might have done a lot of commercials in Japan, but it's possible that European clients won't accept that as proper training. You may have to take classes for their market. It's crucial to understand each market's culture and its consumers. Some markets are easier than others. The more you travel the easier it will become to adapt.

INITIAL EXPENDITURE FOR NEW MODELS

As I have said several times in this book, don't spend any money until you have been accepted by an agency. Your agent will advise you what to do and how to arrange such things as portfolios and headsheets. The figures quoted below are approximate. They are intended only as a guide so you will have some idea of what financial outlay you must make to become a model.

Portfolio	$500–$800
Mini-book	$200–$350
Comp-card (B&W—1000 minimum)	$175–$500
Headsheet (B&W)	$75–$200
Model's bag (as listed on p.44)	$1000–$1500
Make-up	$600–$800
Hair accessories	$250–$300
Underwear and hose	$300–$500
Body stocking	$50–$100
Black high heels	$75–$200
Flat shoes	$35–$200
Walking shoes for rounds	$35–$200
Passport	$50
Total	$3345–$5700

FURTHER READING

You will find a wonderful array of books about grooming, health and exercise in your local book store or library, so I have not given any specific reading recommendations on these subjects here. The books I do list below are all "good reads" and will give you more specific insights to the world of modeling.

High Visibility, Martin Stoller, Irving Rein and Philip Kotler (Dodd Mead & Co., 1987)

International Talent and Modeling Agency Directory, Peter Glenn (Peter Glenn Publishing Co., 1988)

The Master Guide to Photography, Michael Langford (Alfred A. Knopf Publishing Co., 1982)

Ogilvy on Advertising, David Ogilvy (Vintage Books, Random House, 1985)

The Third Wave, Alvin Toffler (Bantam Books, 1982)

The World of International Modeling, Eve Matheson (Matheson Publications, Florida, 1987)

Chapter 8 Bibliography

Exercise, Education and Medicine, R.Tait McKenzie (W.B. Saunders Co., Philadelphia and London, 1924)

Human Body Potential, Lulu E. Sweigard (Harper & Row, New York)

Kinesiology of the Human Body Under Normal and Pathological Conditions, Dr Arthur Steindler (Charles C. Thomas, 1955)

Nutrition and Diet Therapy, 9th edition, Proudfoot and Robinson (Macmillan, New York, 1946)

Total Body Fitness, Robert Gajda and Dr Richard Dominguez (Warner Books, New York, 1982)

Literature produced by the American Dietetic Association was also extremely useful in devising the menus featured in the chapter.

CONTRIBUTORS

CURTIS BRACKENBURY

John Curtis Brackenbury is an eighteenth-generation Canadian. He was born in Kapuskasing, Ontario, and throughout his childhood was involved in amateur sports. He played professional hockey for eleven years, which enabled him to branch out into other fields of athletics, such as Hawaii's world-famous Iron Man Triathlon. In 1986 Curtis was chosen as a crew member on *Canada II*, Canada's entry in the Americas Cup, the 12-meter international yacht race. He was also assistant coordinator of fitness for the Canadian sailing program in Australia. In Canberra he interned at the Australian Institute of Sports' Exercise and Physiology Laboratory under Dr Richard Telford. His experience has led to speaking engagements in Australia, the United States and Canada, and to the creation of a consulting corporation which concentrates on the principles of monitoring the efficiency of human performance. Curtis resides with his wife Deborah in the interior of British Columbia on the family ranch.

Curtis Brackenbury
150B Oliver Street
Williams Lake
British Columbia V2G 1L9
Canada

JUDITH GOLD

A professional in the beauty business since 1967, Judith's career has offered her unlimited opportunities. She has been involved in international show production for Redken educational programs, as well as instructing classes in hair design from basic beauty school to state-of-the-art techniques. Represented by Stewart Beauty, Judith has designed hair for motion pictures, television commercials and national print ads for clients such as Anne Klein perfume. Her strongest commitment is to her salon, Judith Gold Incorporated. "Here," Judith says, "we do more than cut hair — we teach our clients how to choose and develop what is best for their own personal style." When models in Chicago need grooming, they go to Judith Gold.

Judith Gold Salon
650 N. Dearborn
Chicago
Illinois 60610
USA

DEBRA LESSIN

Debra is president and owner of D.J. Lessin & Associates, Inc., Certified Public Accountants. The firm provides a wide range of accounting and tax services with primary emphasis on tax planning and compliance for professional, creative and entrepreneurial small businesses and individuals. Debra began her firm in 1984 after eight years of experience in both "Big Eight" public accounting and the corporate sector. She combines her business savvy and technical expertise with a flair for creativity and humor that, for her, makes people the most important aspect of being a CPA — not just the numbers.

Debra Lessin
Suite 504
444 N. Wells
Chicago
Illinois 60610
USA

DARCY McGRATH

Darcy started in the beauty business in 1981 and has acquired extensive experience of make-up for theater, film and print work. Describing her approach to make-up, she says: "In my own search for harmony and self-expression, I have learned not to disguise the real person I am — only to enhance my assets and learn to accept what is natural."

Darcy McGrath
c/o Stewart Beauty
212 W. Superior
Chicago
Illinois 60610
USA

171

ACKNOWLEDGEMENTS

The author and publishers would particularly like to thank Carole White, co-owner of Premier Model Agency in London, for her valuable contributions to the manuscript.

We are also grateful to the following people and agencies, who took the time to talk and kindly allow us to quote their comments:

Jane Alderman, Michael Baird, Rosemary Bennett, Terry Berland, Tom Bien, Gerard Bisignano, Allan Boyd, Brenda Burns, Dr Richard Caleel, Michael Colliander, Rita Craig, John Crosby, Tania Cross, John David, Mary Duffy, Paul David Fisher, Dave Fleishman, Marjorie Graham, Elsa James, Cynthia Joho, Randy Kirby, Jim Kirchman, Tracy Lambert, Stan Malinowski, Peter McClafferty, Leah McCloskey, Rod McNeil, Marita Monet, Richard Noiret, Laura O'Connor, Ann O'Malley, Lee Ann Perry, Huggy Ragnarsson, Michael Ramion, John Rubano, Tony Shepherd, Roy Skillicorn, Jim Streacker, Donna Surges-Tatum, John Swibes, Don Talley, Linda Thompsen, Vanessa Victor, Di Vidos, Amy Vollmer, Paul Wadina, George Weeks, Coral Weigel, John Welzenbach, Andy Westerman, Cela Wise.

L'Agence, Atlanta; Chadwick's Agency, Melbourne; Eileen Green Agency, Hamburg; Elite, Japan, Los Angeles and Paris; Grimme Agency, San Francisco; International Bookings, Madrid; Irene Marie, Fort Lauderdale; Look Models, Milan; Marcella's Studio, Milan; Models One, London; Nova Models, Munich; Page Parkes Agency, Dallas; Bruce Parker Agency, Toronto; Premier Models, London; Satorou, Osaka; Vivien's Agency, Sydney.

The author also extends special thanks to her "guardian angels": the London "crew" – Chris Owen, Pippa Rubinstein, Anne Fisher, Trish Burgess and Dragon's World staff; the New York "crew" – Allan Lang and John Duff; the Chicago "crew" – J. Cortland Boyd, Jane Stewart, Stan Malinowski, Donna Surges-Tatum, Rita Craig, Rick Cirignani, Dave Fleishman, Bill Graham, the Elite staff and the Stewart Talent staff. Warm thanks also to the many other friends and colleagues, too numerous to list here, who gave such generous help and encouragement.

PHOTOGRAPHY CREDITS

Lack of space prevents all participants being named alongside their photographs. Nonetheless, the following people's talent and professionalism are gratefully acknowledged.

Page 1 Model: Tracy Lambert; Hair/make-up: Jeff O'Hern; Styling: Perry Ventro.
Page 3 Model: Lisa McBride; Make-up/styling: Darcy McGrath.
Page 8 (Left) Models: Steve Wood, Alex Walters and Don Erik (right), courtesy of I. Magnin Co. (Right) Model: Lisa McBride; Styling: Darcy McGrath.
Page 9 (Bottom left) Models: Mary Elking, Jeff Kuri, Paul Wadina, Michael Pawlowski. (Right) Home economist: Lorna Rhodes.
Page 12 Models: Larry Campbell and Russell Warfield.
Pages 14-15 Model: Lizbeth Mustari; Hair/make-up/styling: Felicia Linsky.
Page 17 Model: Tricia Haase.
Page 19 Model: Molly Finn; Hair/make-up: Jeff O'Hern; Styling: Perry Ventro.
Page 20 Model: Michelle Haupert.
Page 27 Models: Lisa Barns, Anthony Vincent; Hair/make-up: Jeff O'Hern.
Page 29 Model: Andrea Robinson.
Page 30 Model: Jeffrey Brezovar.
Page 32 Models: Jill Goodacre (left), Donna Stia (right).
Page 33 Models: Steve Wood; Alex Walters and Don Erik (bottom right), courtesy of I. Magnin Co.
Page 35 Model: Paul Mears.
Page 40-41 Model: Steve Harris; Hair/make-up/styling: Felicia Linsky; model's suit supplied by Davis for Men.
Page 43 Diary supplied by Che Sguardo
Page 44 Stylist: Perry Ventro.
Page 45 (Right) Model: Lizbeth Mustari; Hair/make-up/styling: Felicia Linsky.
Pages 46-47 Stylist: Perry Ventro.
Pages 48-87 All make-up by Darcy McGrath. All hairstyling by Judith Gold.
Pages 48-52 Model: Lisa McBride.
Pages 54-55 Model: Paul Wadina.
Page 57 Model: Lesley Whelan.
Page 58 Model: Lisa McBride.
Page 59 Styling: Darcy McGrath.
Pages 60-65 Model: Mai Strayer.
Page 66 Model: Nicole Berry.
Page 68 Model: Robyn Johnson.
Pages 70-71 Beauty equipment courtesy of Che Sguardo; Styling: Darcy McGrath.
Pages 72-73 Grooming equipment courtesy of Che Sguardo; Styling: Darcy McGrath.
Page 74 Model: Lisa McBride.
Page 75 Model: Carole Kurzin.
Pages 76-77 Models (left to right): Audrey Tom, Tara Mys, Lesley Whelan, Mai Strayer, Michelle Ganales.
Page 77 Model: Mai Strayer.
Pages 78-79 Models (left to right): Carina Asuncion, Michele Meiche, Rita Craig, Kori Nelson, Monique St. Claire.
Pages 82-83 Model: Kate Bracher.
Page 84 Model: Lesley Whelan.

Pages 85-87 Model: Lisa McBride.
Pages 90-91 Model: Kathleen McManamon; Hair/make-up/styling: Felicia Linsky.
Page 94 Models: Jenny George, Caralien Miller, Peggy Johnson, Karen McGlothlin, Mary Pinns; Hair/make-up/styling: Felicia Linsky.
Page 96 Models: Jorie Allen, Kayla Allen, Sean Breen; Hair/make-up: Jeff O'Hern.
Pages 98-99 Models: Stanley Gluck, Amy Vollmer, Caralien Miller, Steve Wood, Vicki Kruse; Hair/make-up/styling: Felicia Linsky.
Page 100 Model: Michael Colliander.
Page 101 Model: Melissa Spring.
Page 102 Model: Amy Vollmer.
Page 103 Model: Caralien Miller.
Page 104 Model: Monique St. Claire; Hair/make-up/styling: Jeff O'Hern.
Page 105 Models (clockwise from top left): Rita Craig, Mei-Li, Don Talley, Elsa James, Anthony Jones.
Page 106 Model: Vicki Kruse.
Page 107 Models: Cindy Waite (bottom left). Jeffrey Brezovar (right).
Pages 108-9 Model: Kelly Killoren; Hair/make-up: Jeff O'Hern; Styling: Perry Ventro.
Page 110 Model: Cindy Waite.
Page 111 Model: Gerry Weitz; Hair: Judith Gold; Styling: David Irving; Client: David & Lee. Originally commissioned by *Metro* magazine.
Page 112 (Bottom left) Originally commissioned by Ogilvy Mather advertising agency; Art director: Barbara Travis. (Bottom right) Originally commissioned by Bozell, Jacobs, Kenyon & Eckhardt, Inc.; Client: Contel Telephone Operations; Art director: Kent Ottwell; Model: Irene Best; Hair/make-up: Cindy Adams; Stylist: Diane Pronites.
Page 113 Originally commissioned by Frankenberry Laughlin Constible; Art director: Kathy Sherwood; Styling: Francine Gourguechon.
Page 114 Originally commissioned by J. Walter Thompson advertising agency; Model: Brenda Burns.

Page 116 (Top left) Cathy Gallegen. (Right) Ally Dunn.
Page 117 Model: Liza Graham.
Page 119 Model: Brian Terrell.
Page 120 Model: Dana Nemer.
Page 124 Model: Nancy Decker; Hair: Bruno; Make-up: Sophie Levy; Art editor; Carla Engler.
Page 125 Model: Kelly Emberg; Hair: Bruno; Make-up: Sophie Levy; Art editor: Carla Engler.
Page 129 Model: Julie Foster.
Pages 130-31 Model: Bridget Etzkorn.
Page 135 Models: Mary Elking, Jeff Kuri, Paul Wadina, Michael Pawlowski.
Page 136 Art directors: Jo Hoddy, Liz O'Connor.
Page 138 Model: Ashley Quirco.
Page 139 Model: Cindy Crawford.
Page 140 Model: Stephanie Averill; Hair/make-up/styling: Felicia Linsky.
Pages 144-47 Home economist: Lorna Rhodes.
Page 148 Model: Lynn Kempton.
Page 149 Model: Deborah Armstrong.
Page 151 Models: Lynn Kempton, Jack McIntosh.
Pages 152-54 Model: Lynn Kempton.
Page 155 Model: Cari Saloch.
Pages 156-57 Model: Molly Finn; Hair/make-up: Jeff O'Hern; Styling: Perry Ventro. Shot on location at City Store by kind permission of the management.
Pages 164-65 Acting instructor: Di Vidos; Models: Ylwa Warghusen, Maya Saxton.
Page 168 John Rubano.
Page 169 Beth Behrends. Hair/make-up: Bob Pitts.
Page 173 Model: Lisa McBride; Styling: Darcy McGrath.

While every effort has been made to ensure the accuracy of these credits, the publishers invite readers to bring any errors or omissions to their attention so that they can be corrected in future editions of the book.

STEPHEN WOLTER

INDEX

Figures in italic type denote photographs.

175